Early SPACE Encyclopedias

THE SUN

by Megan Borgert-Spaniol

Early Encyclopedias

An Imprint of Abdo Reference
abdobooks.com

abdobooks.com

Published by Abdo Reference, a division of ABDO, PO Box 398166, Minneapolis, Minnesota 55439.

Printed in China.
102025
012026

Editor: Arnold Ringstad
Series Designers: Candice Keimig, Joshua Olson
Production Designer: Ryan Gale

Library of Congress Control Number: 2025939291

Publisher's Cataloging-in-Publication Data

Names: Borgert-Spaniol, Megan, author.
Title: The sun / by Megan Borgert-Spaniol
Description: Minneapolis, Minnesota: Abdo Reference, 2026 | Series: Early space encyclopedias | Includes online resources and index.
Identifiers: ISBN 9781098298814 (lib. bdg.) | ISBN 9798384932611 (ebook)
Subjects: LCSH: Outer space--Exploration--Juvenile literature. | Astronomy--Juvenile literature. | Solar System--Juvenile literature. | Sun--Juvenile literature. | Stars--Juvenile literature. | Sky--Juvenile literature. | Encyclopedias--Juvenile literature.
Classification: DDC 523.7--dc23

CONTENTS

The sun's bright light shines on Earth from millions of miles away.

What Is the Sun?

People can see thousands of stars at night. But just one is visible during the day. This is the sun.

Like all stars, the sun is a hot ball of gas. The sun is the nearest star. It is about 93 million miles (150 million km) from Earth.

The Solar System

The solar system includes the sun and all the nearby objects around it. The sun is the solar system's largest object. It has 330,000 times Earth's mass. About 1.3 million Earths could fit inside the sun.

The sun is far larger than Earth and the other planets.

The Sun's Gravity

The sun's large mass means it has powerful gravity. Gravity is a force. Earth's gravity pulls objects to the planet's surface. The sun's gravity pulls at the planets. This force makes Earth and the other planets orbit, or go around, the sun.

The sun's powerful gravity holds all the planets in place.

Heat and Light

The sun provides heat and light. Humans couldn't survive without it. In fact, the sun makes life on Earth possible.

HOW THE SUN FORMED

Stars are born in huge clouds of dust and gas.

Gas and Dust

The sun formed more than 4.5 billion years ago. It began as a cloud of gas and dust. Then a nearby star exploded. This sent waves of energy through the cloud. The energy caused the cloud to rotate.

A Flat Disk

The spinning cloud became flat like a disk. At the center was a ball of hydrogen and helium. These gases heated up as they got closer together. This took millions of years.

Gravity pulls together the gases that will become a star.

Nuclear Fusion

The heat caused hydrogen atoms to fuse. This means pairs of atoms joined together. Each pair of hydrogen atoms became a helium atom. This process is called nuclear fusion. It creates heat and light. With the start of nuclear fusion, the sun became a star.

When fusion begins, a star starts to give off energy.

The planets formed millions of years after the sun.

Forming Planets

Some gas and dust remained from the original cloud. These things formed clumps. These clumps became the solar system's planets and moons.

Today's scientists are learning more about distant stars and planets.

Stars Beyond

There are billions of stars outside the solar system. Many are part of their own planetary systems. This means planets orbit them.

Average Star

The size of the sun is average compared with other stars. Scientists have found stars up to 100 times larger. They have also found stars ten times smaller.

Comparing Stars

The sun is known as a yellow dwarf star. Red dwarf stars such as Wolf 359 are smaller and cooler than the sun. Blue supergiant stars such as Rigel are bigger and hotter.

Sun

Wolf 359

Sun

Rigel

Hydrogen and Helium

About 75 percent of the sun's mass is hydrogen. Hydrogen is the lightest chemical element. About 25 percent of the star's mass is helium. It is the second-lightest element.

Hydrogen and helium are very light gases. They have been used to make airships float through the sky.

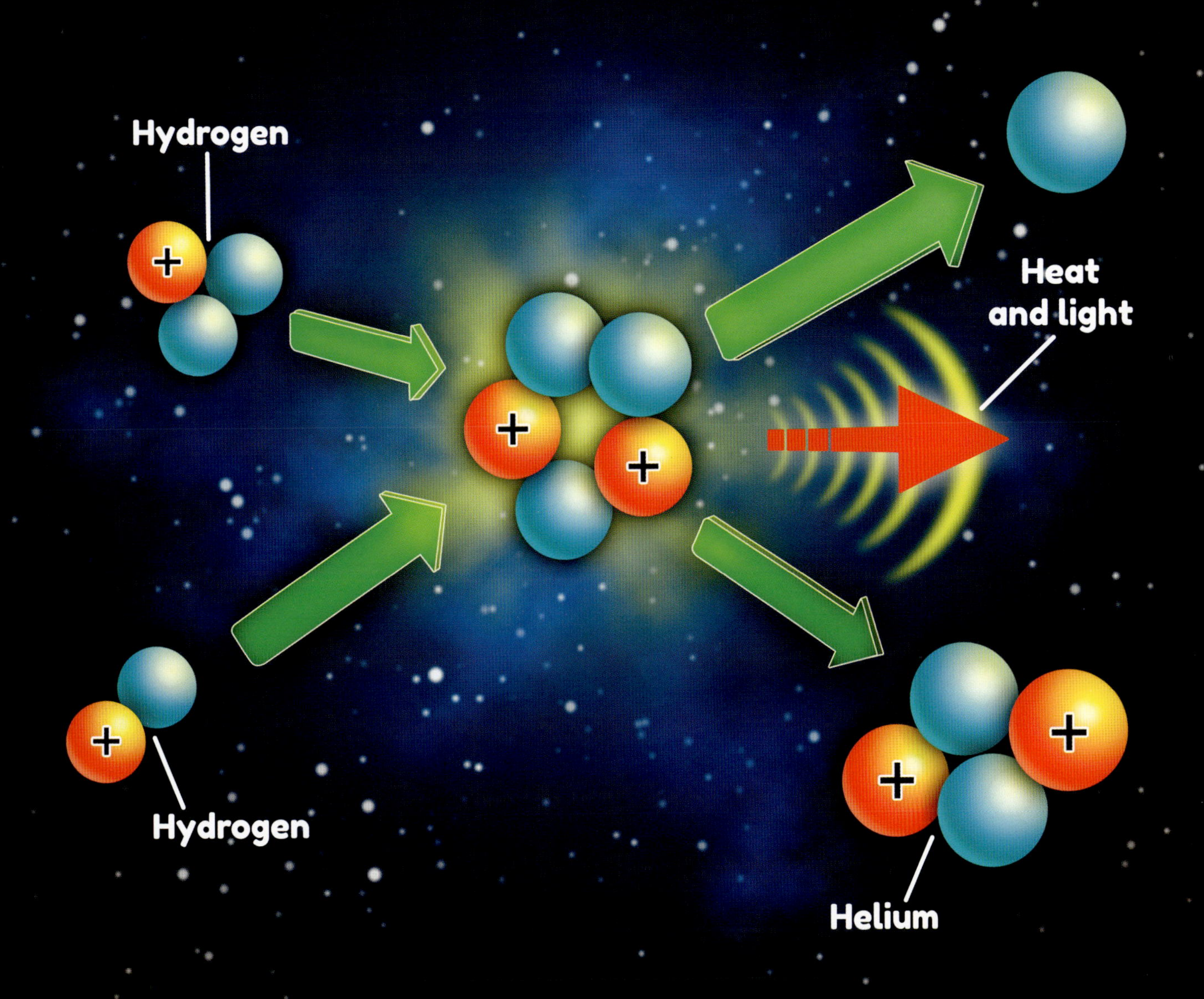

Hydrogen atoms fuse together deep inside the sun.

Fusing Together

Nuclear fusion happens in the sun's core. The process gives off heat and light. It has been happening for billions of years.

Metals such as iron are found in the sun as well as on Earth.

Other Elements

The sun also has other elements. Some are metals. They include iron and magnesium. Others are nonmetals. These include oxygen and carbon.

Small but Massive

These other elements make up only about 2 percent of the sun's mass. But the sun is huge. These elements total more than 5,000 times the mass of Earth.

Elements of the Sun

Scientists have identified more than 60 chemical elements in the sun.

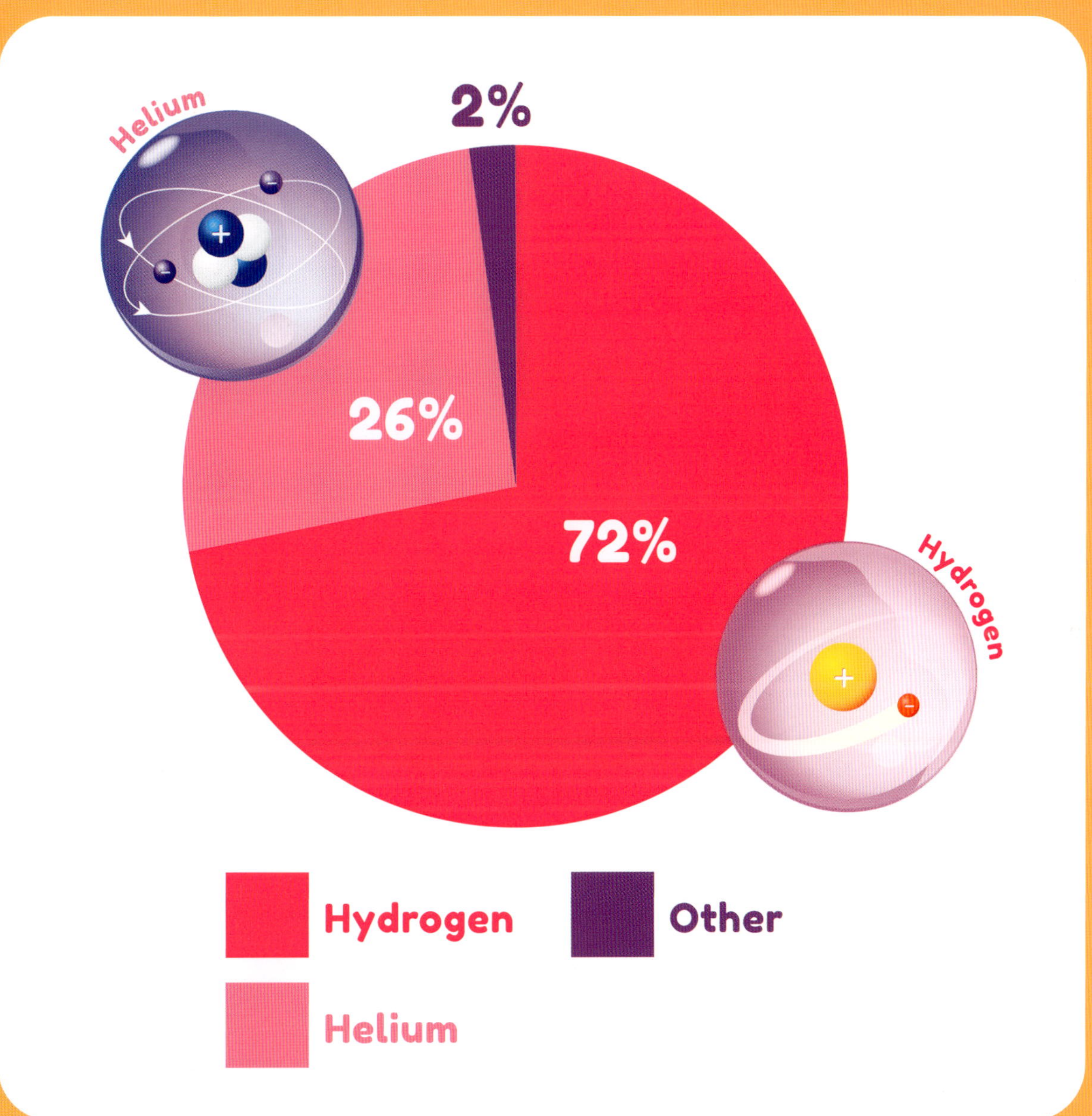

Layers of the Sun

The sun has inner and outer layers. The inner layers are the core, radiative zone, and convection zone. The outer layers are the photosphere, chromosphere, and corona.

The sun has six main layers.

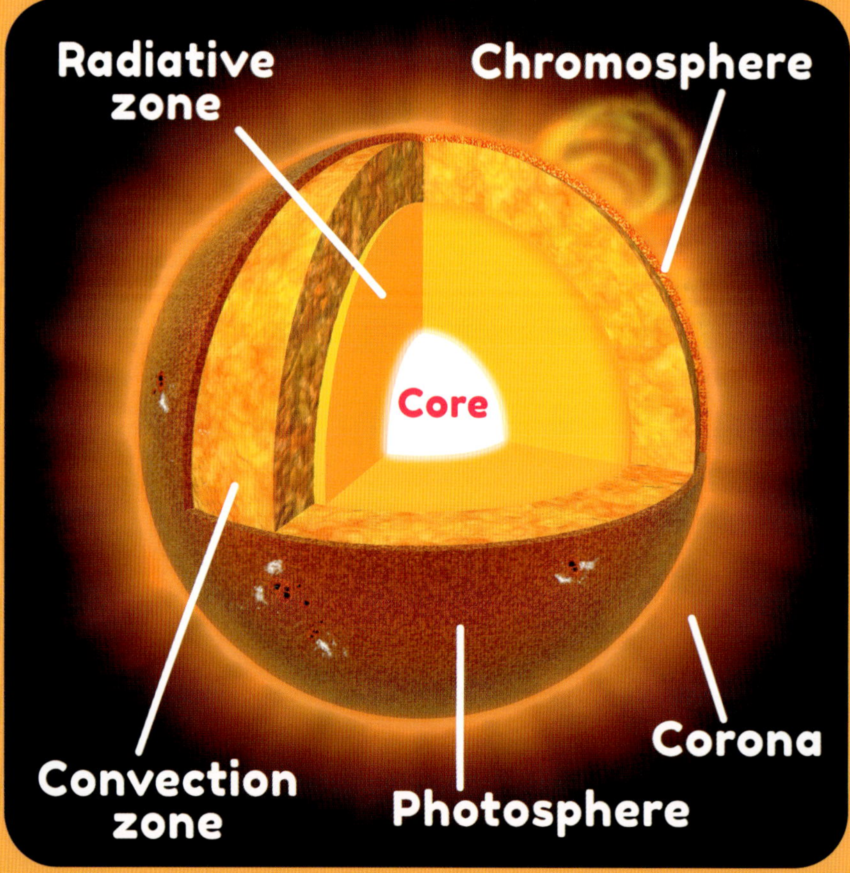

Energy produced deep inside the sun reaches Earth after a long time.

Core

The core is the innermost layer. It is also the hottest. Temperatures reach 27 million degrees Fahrenheit (15 million°C). The core is where nuclear fusion happens.

FUN FACT!

The sun gives off more energy in one second than Earth uses in a year.

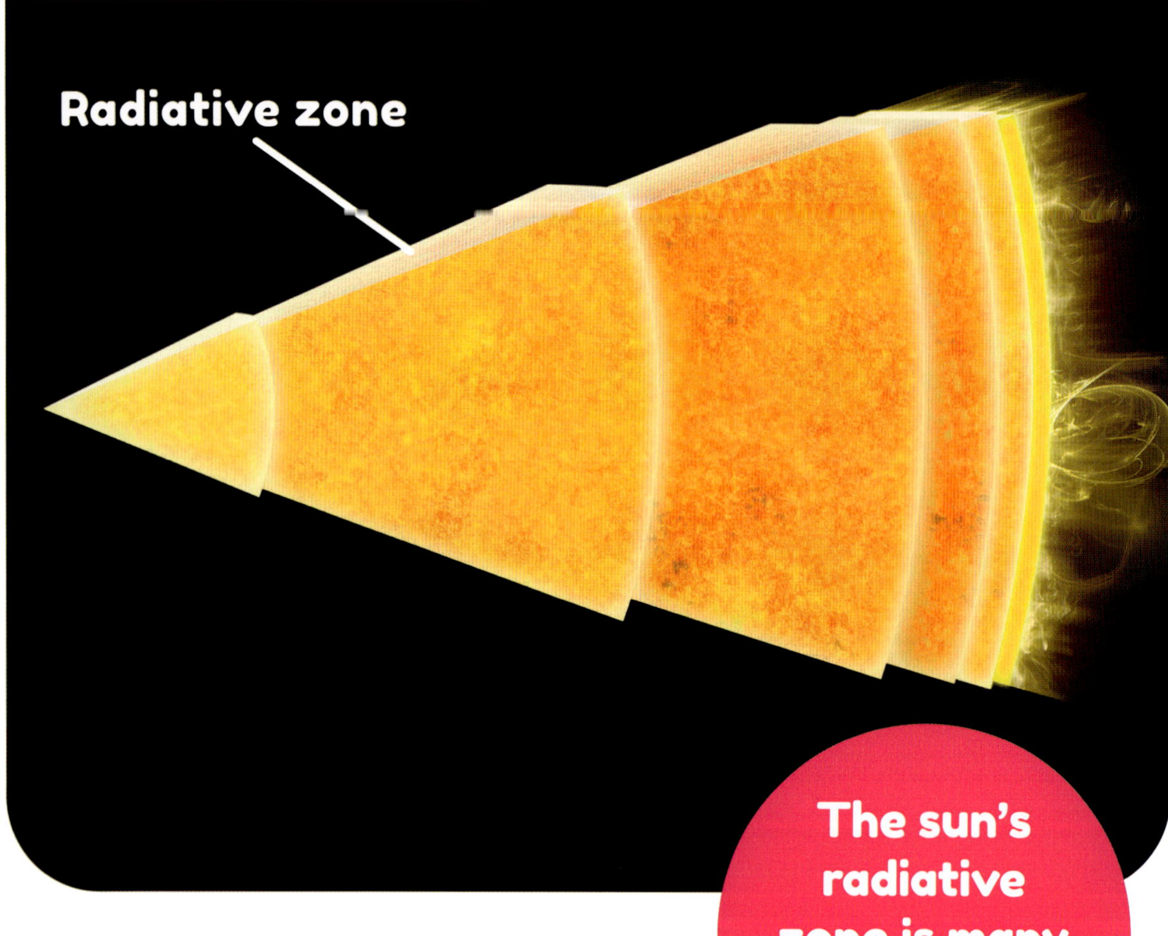

The sun's radiative zone is many thousands of miles thick.

Radiative Zone

Next is the radiative zone. The temperature is 4 million degrees Fahrenheit (2.2 million°C). Energy from the core moves out through the radiative zone. This energy is called radiation.

FUN FACT!

Photons travel about 186,000 miles per second (300,000 km/s).

Photons

Radiation is made up of tiny packets of energy called photons. These photons move through the sun's layers. Their path is not straight. They bump into particles along the way. It can take photons a million years to move through the radiative zone.

Photons leave the sun after traveling through all of its layers.

Convection Zone

The next layer is the convection zone. The temperature is 3.5 million degrees Fahrenheit (1.9 million°C). Gases rise through this layer. Then they cool down. This makes the gases sink. They heat up again in the lower part of this layer.

Gases are always moving around in the convection zone.

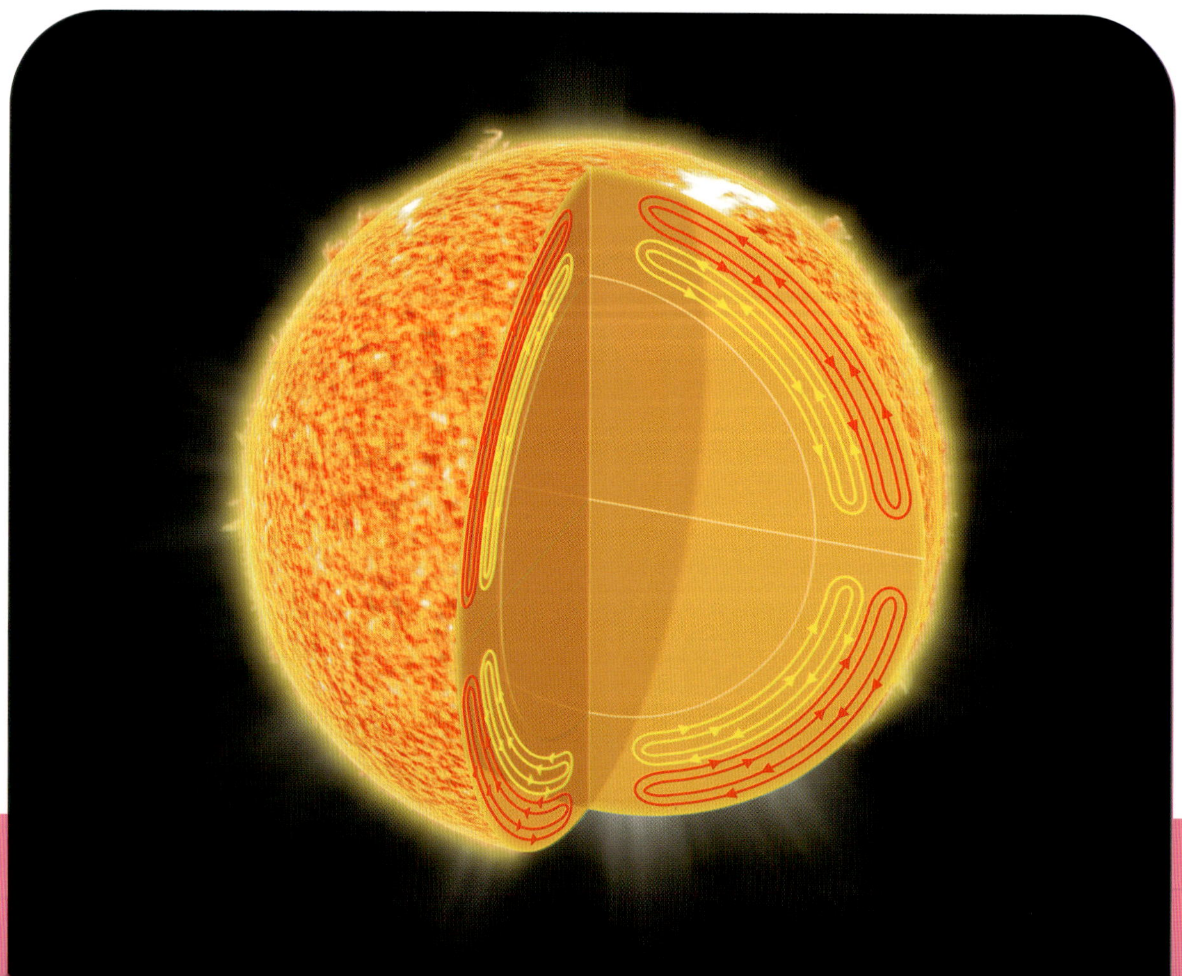

More about Convection

Gases in the convection zone behave like boiling water. The water rises up and away from the stove. Then it cools and sinks back down to be heated again. This movement of heat is known as convection.

FUN FACT!

The term *photosphere* means "sphere of light."

People can observe the photosphere using special telescopes.

Photosphere

Next comes the photosphere.
This is the surface of the sun. The photosphere is about 250 miles (400 km) thick. The temperature is about 10,300 degrees Fahrenheit (5,700°C). The photosphere gives off most of the sun's visible light. It is the part people see from Earth.

Granules

The photosphere has spots called granules. Brighter spots show rising gas. Darker ones show sinking gas. Granules look tiny from Earth. But they are hundreds of miles wide.

Close-up photos of the sun reveal granules.

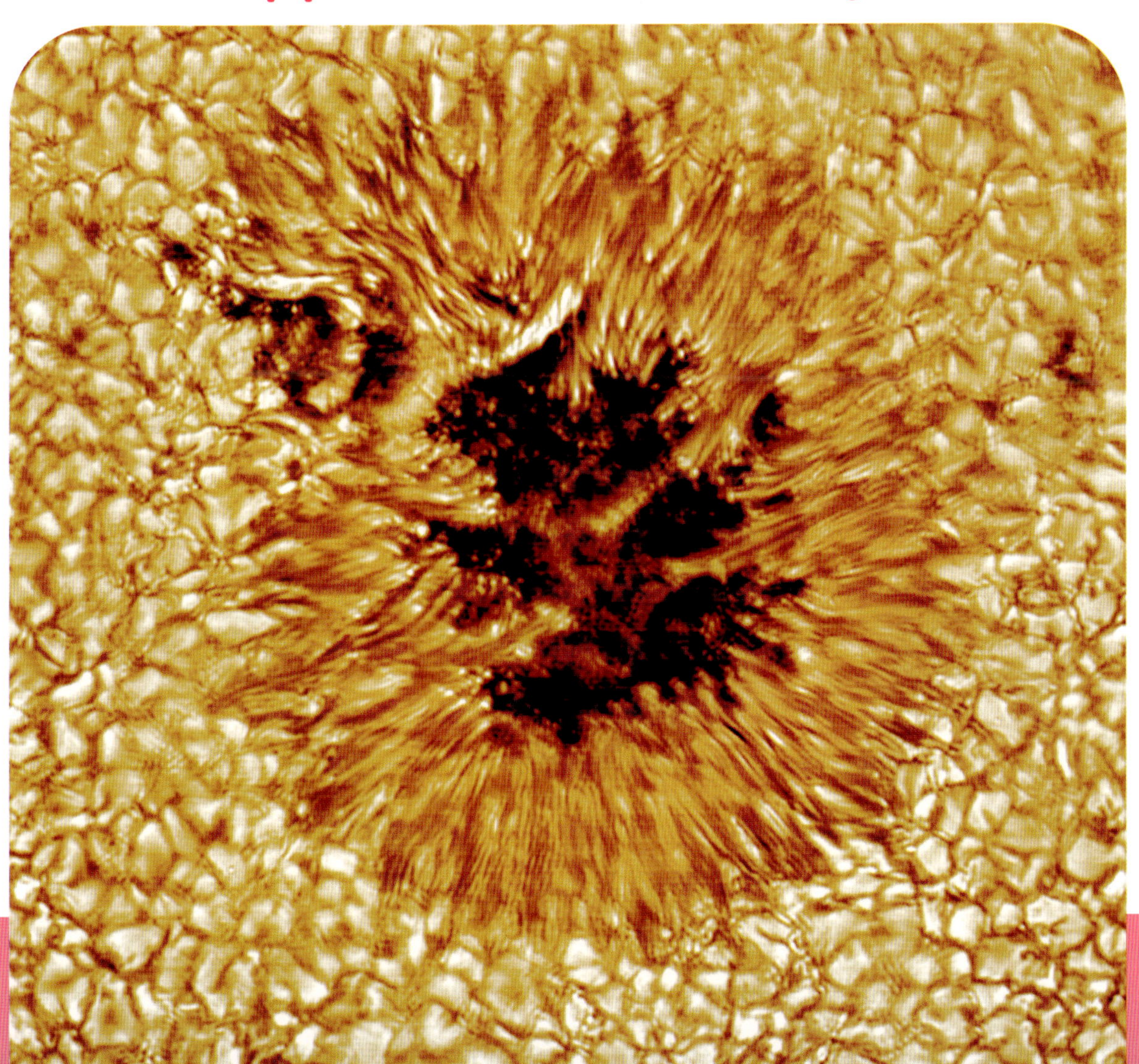

Chromosphere

Next is the chromosphere. This layer stretches about 1,250 miles (2,000 km) above the surface. It is made up of thin jets of hot gas. The chromosphere gives off a reddish glow. It is hard to see because the sun is so bright.

The chromosphere can be seen around the edges of the sun.

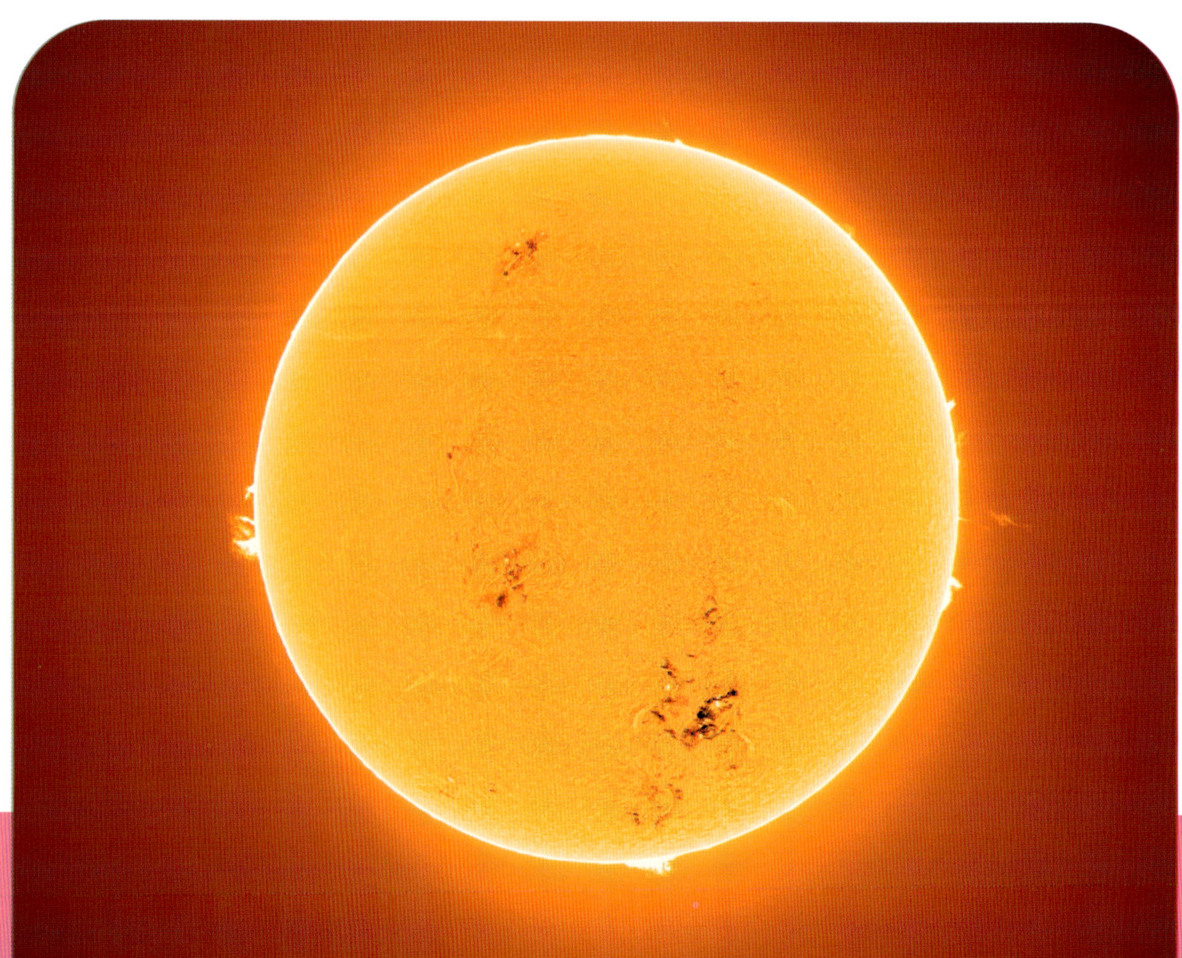

Jets of gas miles long are visible in the chromosphere.

Varying Temperature

Temperatures vary in the chromosphere. They are around 7,500 degrees Fahrenheit (4,100°C) in the lower areas. Higher areas rise to 45,000 degrees Fahrenheit (25,000°C).

The corona extends far into space.

Corona

The outermost layer is the corona. Temperatures rise sharply here. This layer reaches 3.5 million degrees Fahrenheit (1.9 million°C).

The Sun's Crown

Corona means "crown." Streams of gas reach into space. They look like the points of a crown. These gases travel about 90 miles per second (145 km/s).

A Burning Question

The corona is far from the sun's core. So why is this layer so hot? This is a mystery that scientists are still trying to understand.

The corona can be seen during a solar eclipse.

Plasma

The sun's gases are so hot that they become plasma. Plasma is similar to gas. But its particles have an electric charge.

FUN FACT!

Plasma is the most common state of matter in the universe.

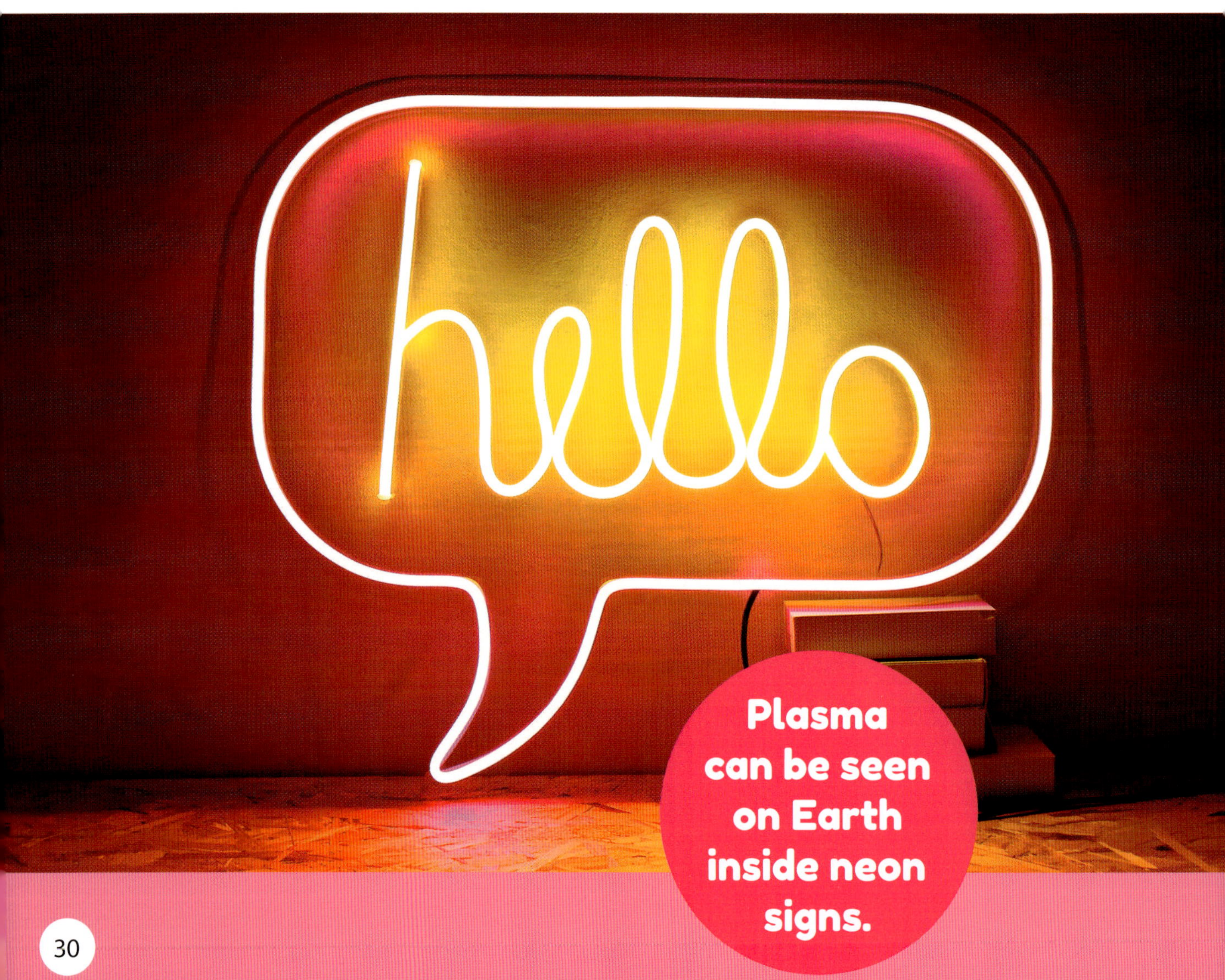

Plasma can be seen on Earth inside neon signs.

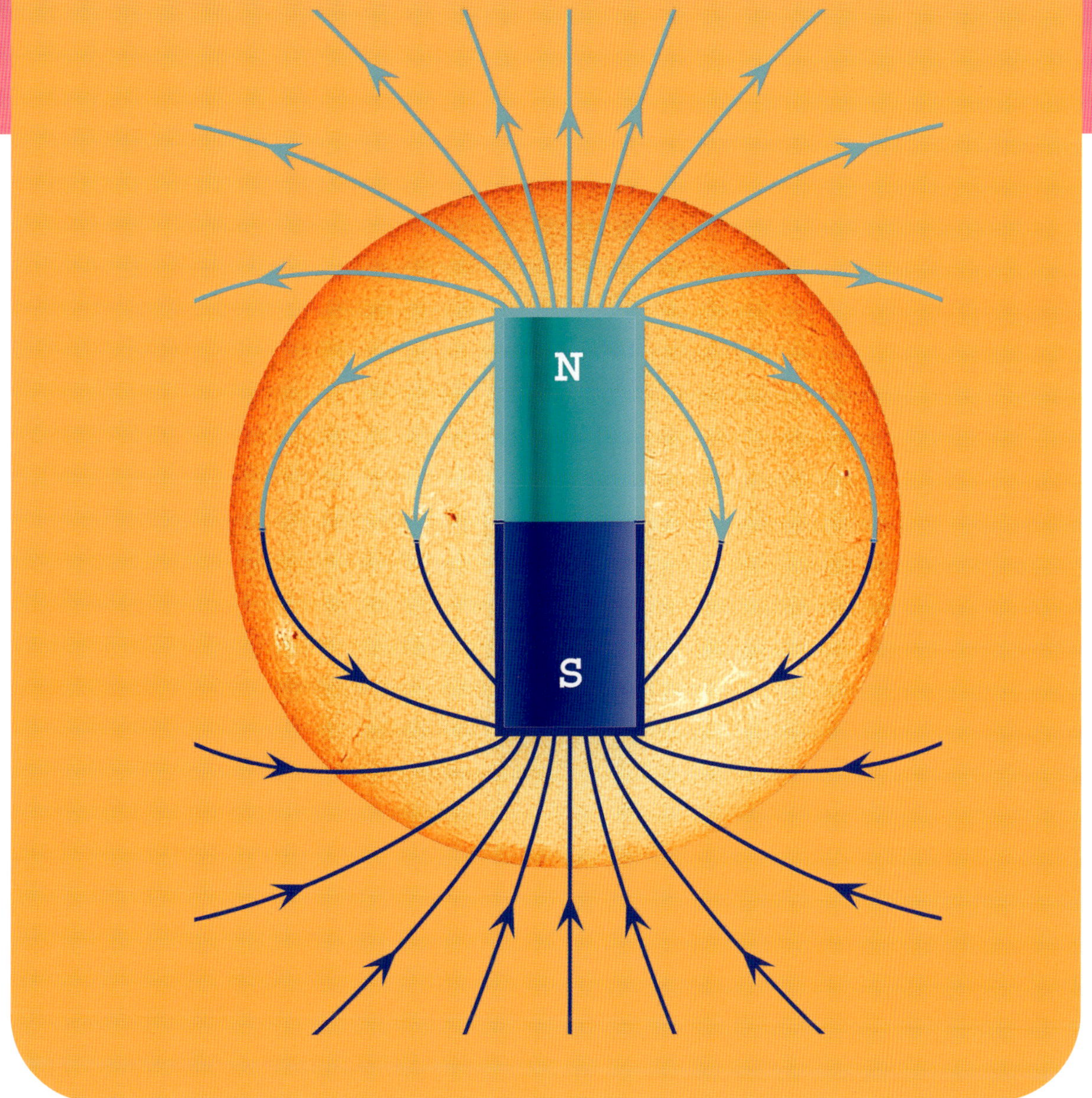

Like a magnet, the sun has north and south poles.

Electric and Magnetic

Moving plasma particles create electric currents. These electric currents form a magnetic field. This means the sun acts like a huge magnet.

Solar wind streams out from the sun toward the planets.

Solar Wind

Some plasma particles move at high speeds. They go fast enough to escape the sun's gravity. This is called solar wind.

Heliosphere

Solar wind blows out from the sun. These charged particles carry the sun's magnetic field into space. This forms a huge magnetic bubble called the heliosphere.

FUN FACT!

The heliosphere stretches across the solar system. It protects Earth and other planets from radiation from outer space.

Scientists created this map of the heliosphere.

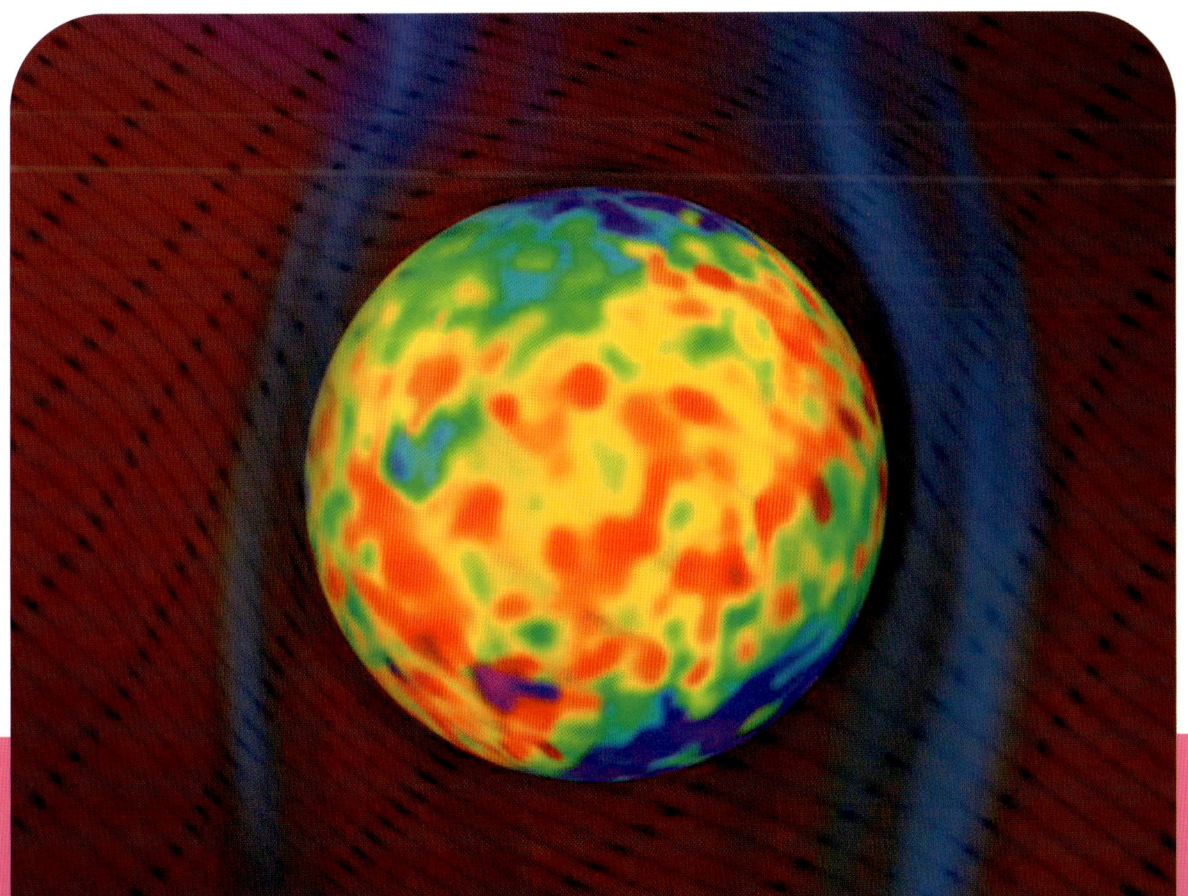

Solar Cycle

The sun's magnetic field causes activity on the sun's surface. This activity varies over the course of about 11 years. This time period is known as the solar cycle.

It may not be apparent from Earth, but the sun's surface is always changing.

During periods of low activity, there may be no sunspots for days at a time.

Solar Activity

During part of the solar cycle, the sun's magnetic poles flip around. This time has high solar activity. Solar activity includes sunspots, solar flares, and more.

Sunspots

Sunspots are cooler areas of the surface. They result from strong magnetic activity. Sunspots last from days to months.

Sunspots are small dark areas on the sun.

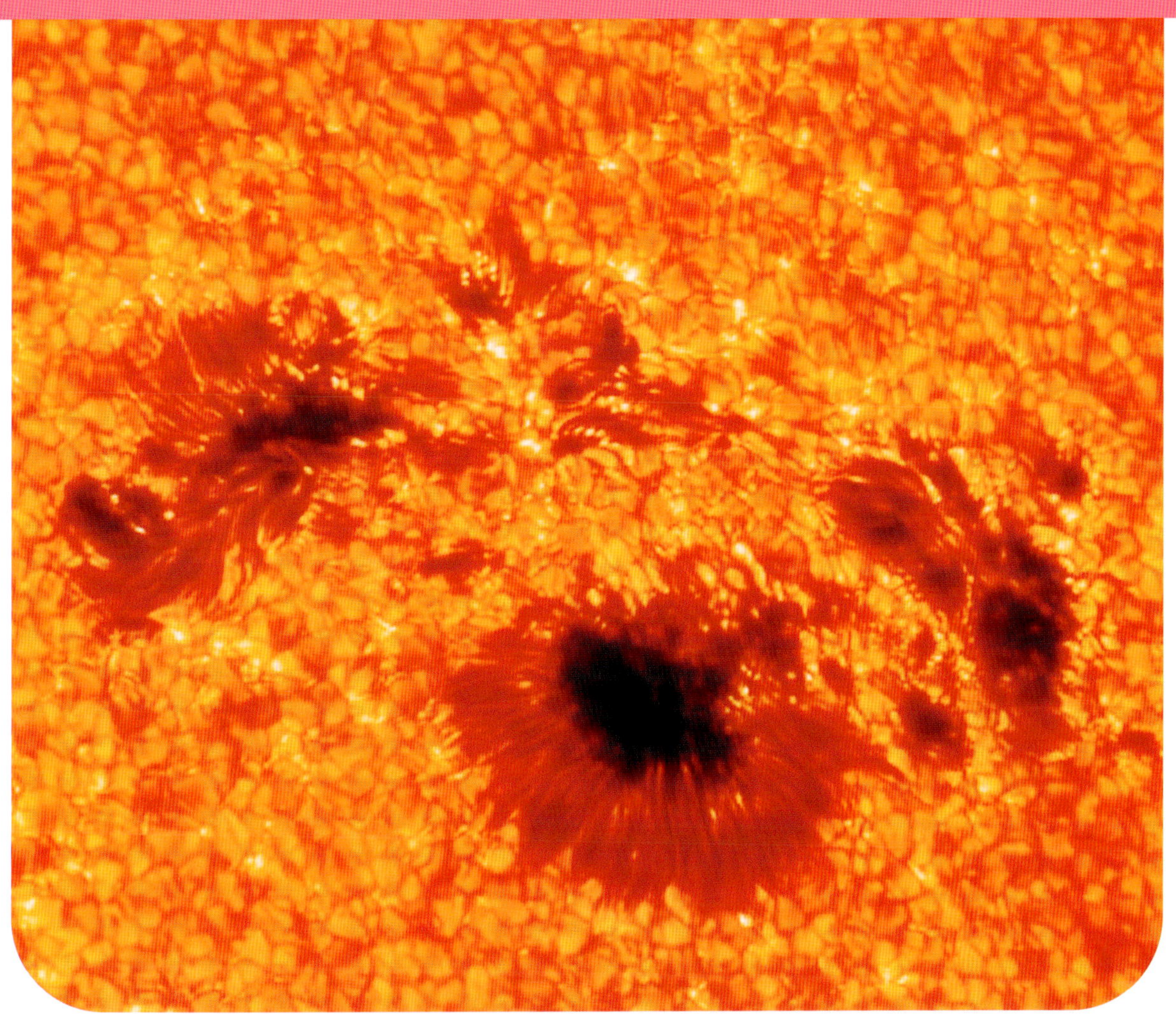

Powerful telescopes show detailed views of sunspots.

Supersized

Through telescopes, sunspots appear as dark spots. They look like small freckles. But they are actually thousands of miles across.

Scientists observed this bright solar flare in 2014.

Solar Flares

Solar flares are big explosions of radiation. They usually occur near sunspots. Solar flares look like flashes of light. They can last for hours.

Power Packed

Solar flares are the most powerful explosions in the solar system. Some have the energy of a billion hydrogen bombs. That's enough energy to power Earth for 20,000 years.

A 2023 image shows multiple bright flashes on the sun.

Solar Prominences

A prominence is something that sticks out from something else. Solar prominences are bright loops of plasma. They rise from the sun's surface. The sun's magnetic field holds them in place. Prominences last up to a few months.

Solar prominences can be seen along the sun's edge.

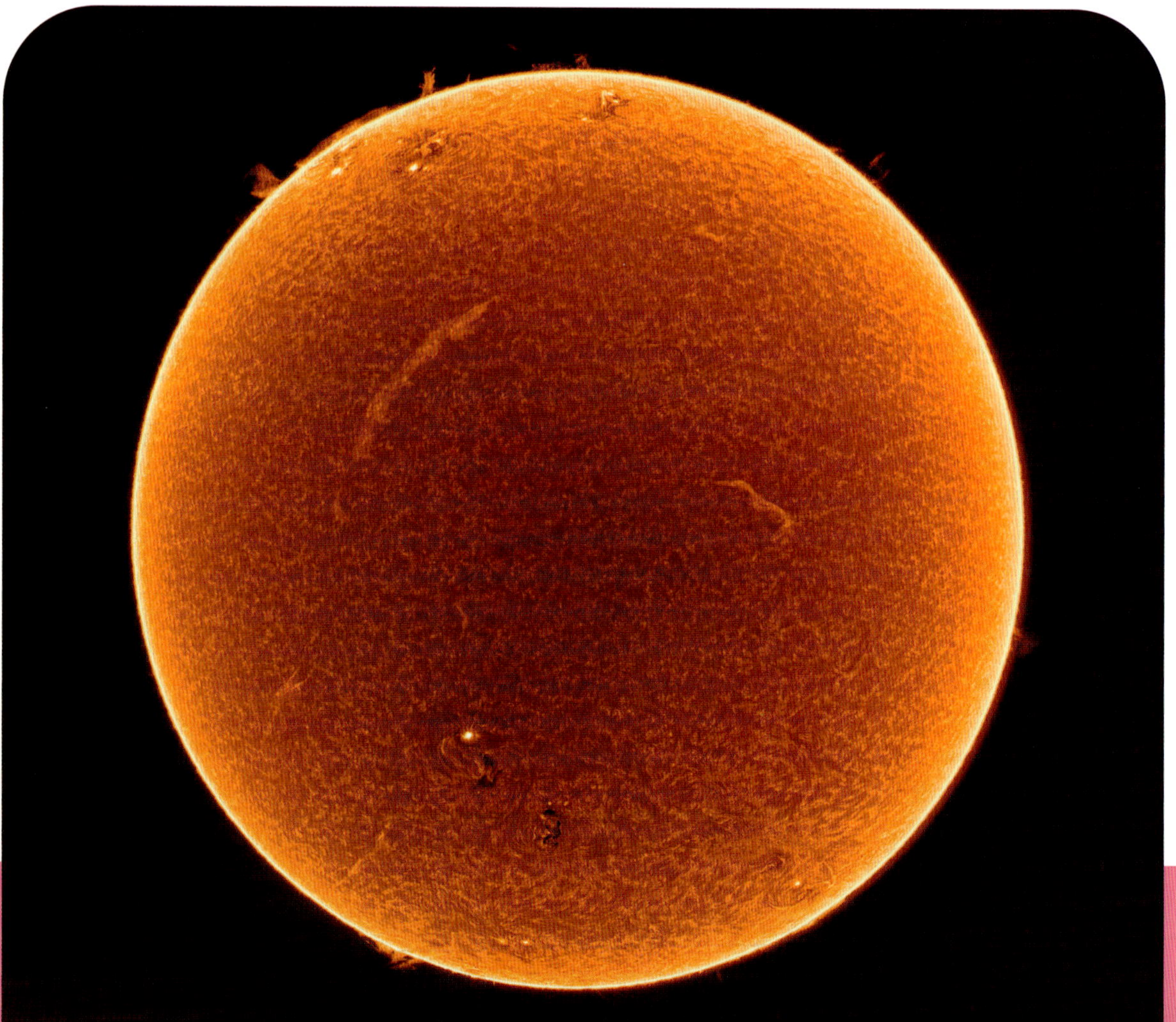

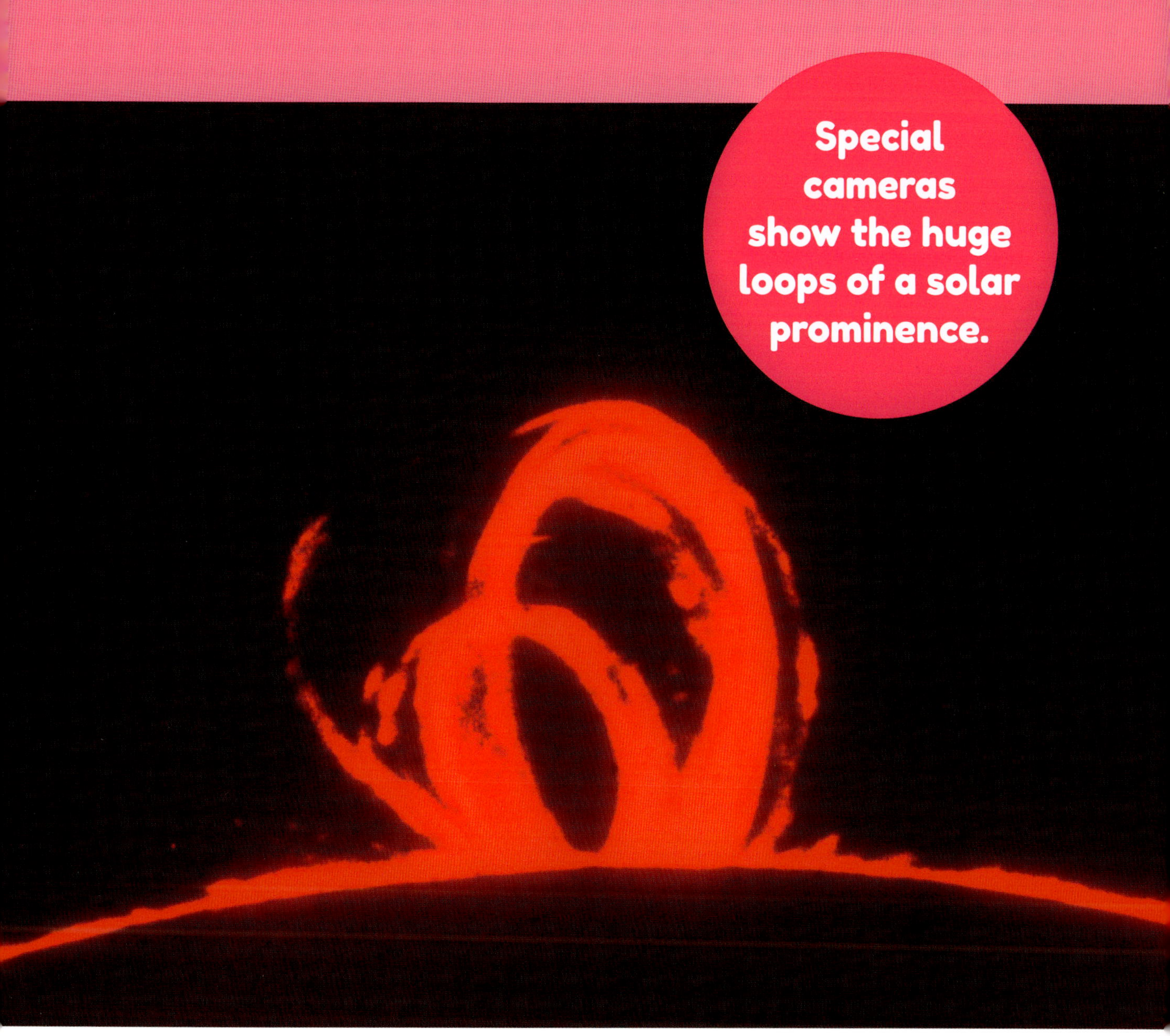

Flaming Arches

Prominences look like arching flames. These arches reach many thousands of miles high. Dozens of Earths could fit under a prominence.

CMEs blast into space from the sun's surface.

Coronal Mass Ejections

A coronal mass ejection is also known as a CME. It is a giant cloud of plasma. It erupts from the sun. CMEs often occur along with solar flares.

Burning Bubbles

CMEs erupt at more than 1 million miles per hour (1.6 million km/h). They grow to millions of miles wide. CMEs look like burning bubbles.

A NASA image shows a solar flare and CME pointed directly at Earth.

Light

The sun's light makes life on Earth possible. Plants take in light. They use it to make their own food. This lets them survive and grow. The energy is passed on to animals that eat the plants.

FUN FACT!

It takes about 8 minutes for light to travel from the sun to Earth.

From a tall tree to a blade of grass, all plants need sunlight.

Heat

The sun's heat also makes life possible. The sun keeps Earth warm. Without the sun's heat, Earth would quickly freeze. It would become too cold for life.

In astronomy, the line between day and night is called the terminator.

Day and Night

Only half of Earth faces the sun at a time. This side experiences daytime. On the side facing away from the sun, it's nighttime.

24 Hours

Earth is always rotating. It takes 24 hours to make one full turn. In that time, the world experiences one day and one night.

First Sunrise

The sun rises in the east. This means that Maine is the first US state to see the sunrise each day.

Day begins as the sun rises above the horizon.

The Tides

The ocean's surface rises and falls. This creates changing water levels called tides. The gravity of the sun and moon causes Earth's tides.

High and Low

In some areas, this gravity pulls water away from Earth. This causes high tides in these places. Other parts of the planet experience low tides.

The sun's gravity and the moon's gravity pull at the ocean's surface.

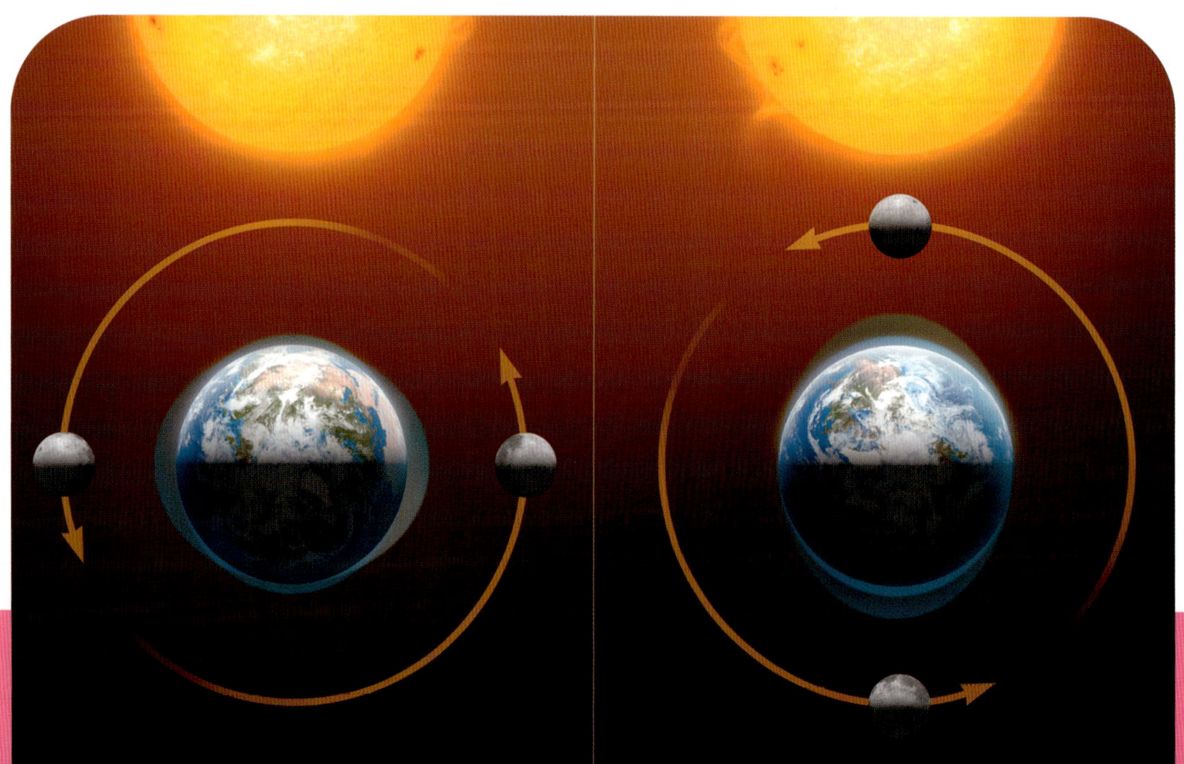

People
can track
and forecast
the tides.

Sunny days are more common in some parts of the world than in others.

Uneven Heating

The sun heats Earth's surface unevenly. This is partly because Earth is tilted. Some parts get more direct sunlight than others. Heat also affects land and water differently. Land heats up faster than water.

Wind

When land heats up, the air above it becomes less dense. This causes the air to rise. Cooler, denser air takes its place. This movement of air creates wind.

One Year

As Earth rotates, it also orbits around the sun. It takes about 365 days for Earth to orbit the sun one time. This is the length of a year.

Earth's rotation causes sunrises and sunsets.

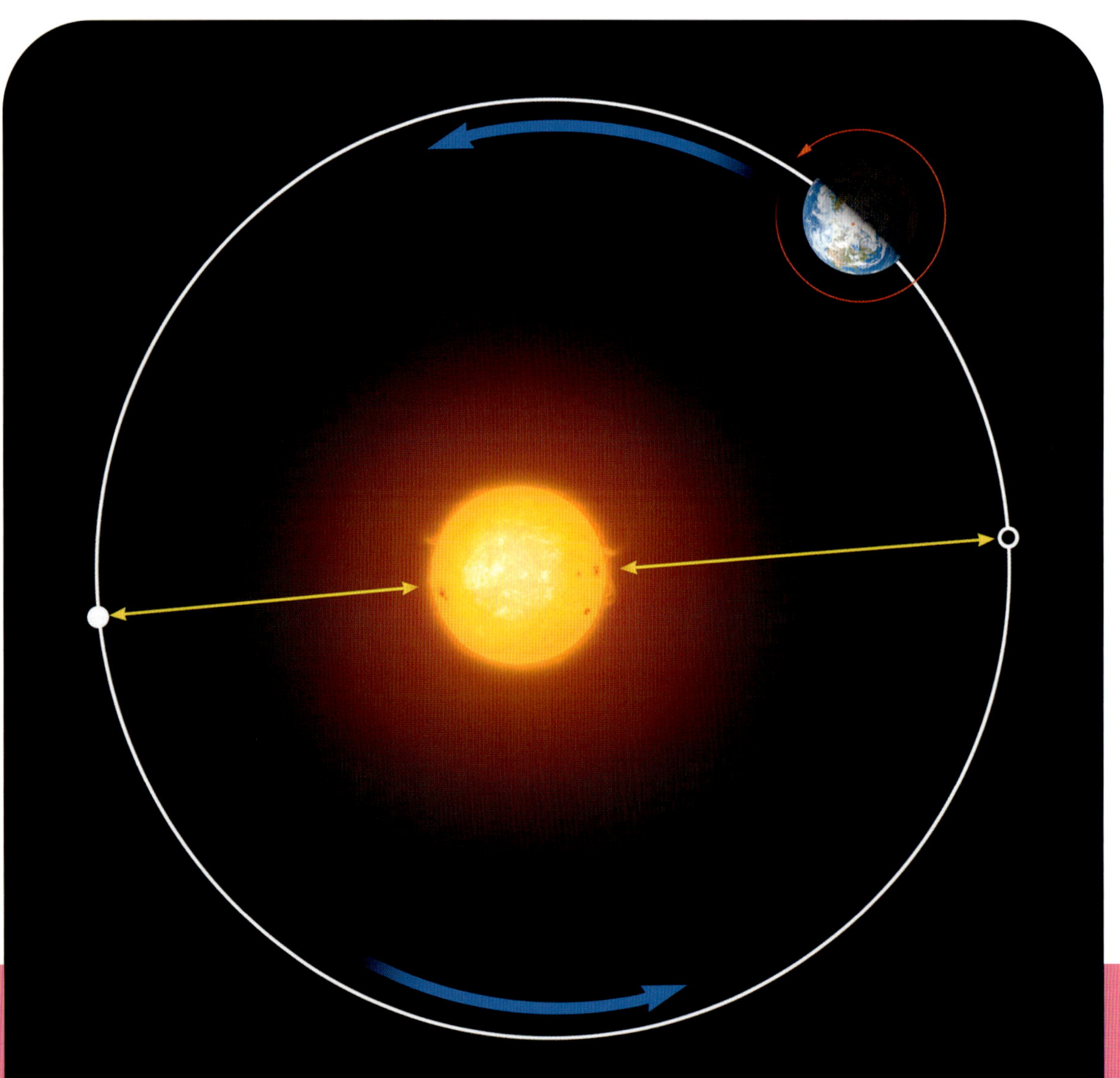

The year 2024 was a leap year, so it included February 29.

Leap Year

It actually takes Earth 365 days and 6 hours to go around the sun. The extra 6 hours add up to a full day every four years. That's why every fourth year has 366 days. These years are known as leap years.

February 29

The extra day in a leap year is added to the month of February. In these years, February has 29 days instead of 28.

Earth is tilted at an angle of 23.5 degrees.

Seasons

Earth's Northern Hemisphere tilts toward the sun in the hemisphere's summer. It later tilts away from the sun. This time is winter.

North and South

The Northern and Southern Hemispheres experience opposite seasons. When it's summer in the north, it's winter in the south. The Southern Hemisphere is tilted away from the sun at that time.

Seasons are caused by Earth's tilt.

Midnight Sun

The sun never sets during summer at the North Pole. That's because this region faces the sun 24 hours a day.

Summer Solstice

Each year has two solstices. The summer solstice is the longest day of the year. This day gets more hours of sunlight than any other day. In the Northern Hemisphere, this day is in June.

New York City is in the Northern Hemisphere. Summer begins in June on this half of Earth.

Winter Solstice

The winter solstice is the shortest day of the year. This day gets fewer hours of sunlight than any other day. In the Northern Hemisphere, this day is in December.

Leaves change colors and the weather cools down during the autumnal equinox.

Equinoxes

Each year also has two equinoxes. On these days, the sun is directly above the equator. Day and night are about the same length.

Spring and Fall

The equinoxes mark the start of spring and fall. Spring starts in March in the Northern Hemisphere. Fall starts in September. The spring equinox is also known as the vernal equinox. The fall equinox is called the autumnal equinox.

Growing plants and warming temperatures are common at the spring equinox.

The Water Cycle

The sun powers the water cycle. This is the movement of water around Earth and its atmosphere. Water is always moving and changing form.

How It Works

The sun heats water on Earth's surface. This makes the water evaporate. It rises into Earth's atmosphere. There it cools and condenses. It forms clouds. These clouds then drop rain and snow to the surface. The cycle begins again.

Water is necessary for life on Earth.

Moving Water

Evaporation is the change from a liquid to a gas. Condensation is the change from a gas to a liquid. And precipitation is water that falls from Earth's atmosphere to its surface.

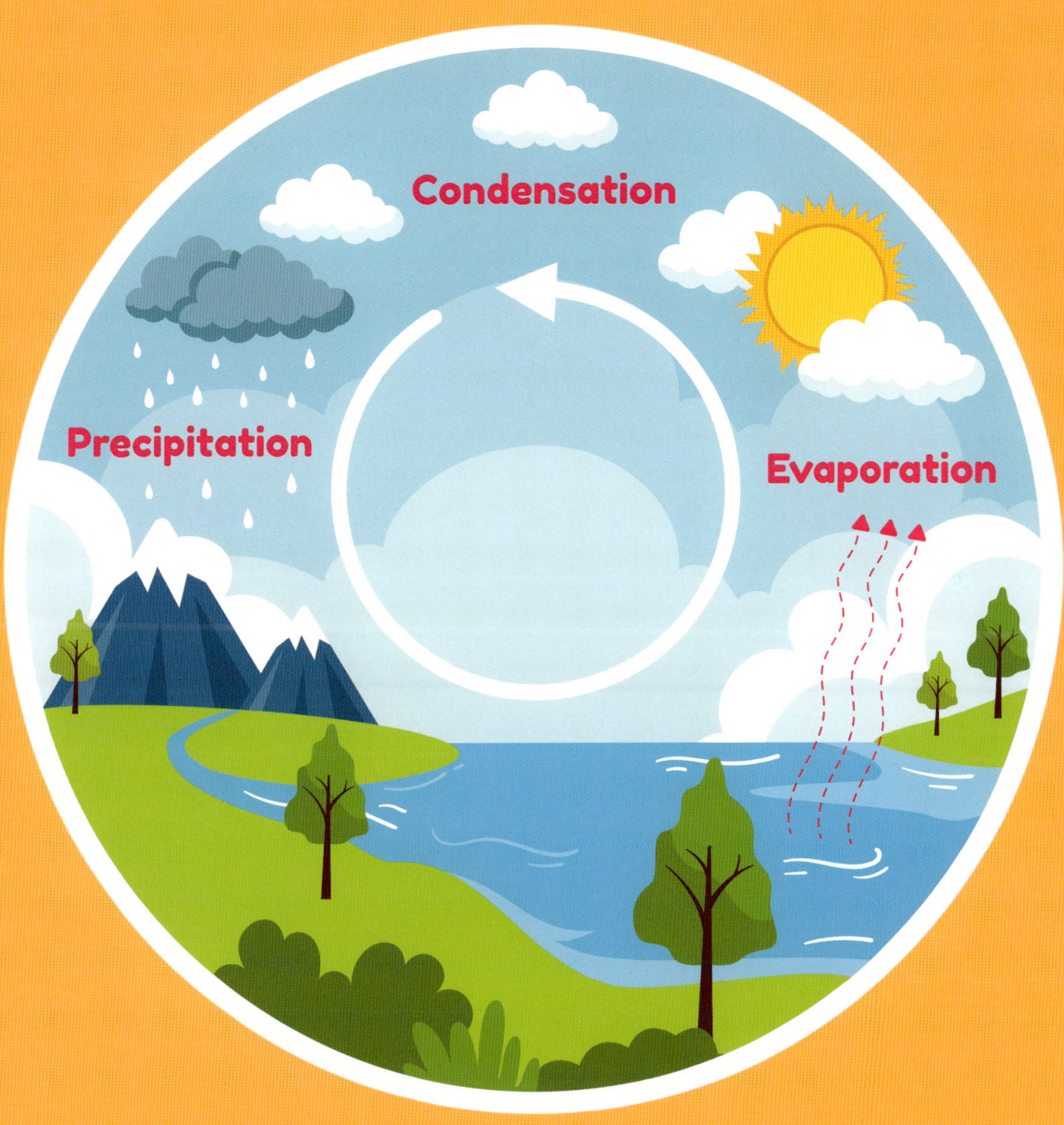

Coal is a solid type of fossil fuel.

Fossil Fuels

Plants take in the sun's energy. After they die, they sink into the ground. Millions of years pass. Heat and pressure change their form. The plants become oil, natural gas, and coal. Humans use these things as fuel. That's why oil, natural gas, and coal are known as fossil fuels.

Using Fossil Fuels

Humans dig up fossil fuels from the ground. They burn the fuels to produce electricity. This uses the energy the plants originally got from the sun.

Oil rigs drill for oil buried under the seafloor.

Nonrenewable Energy

Fossil fuels get used up over time. It takes a long time for more to form. That's why fossil fuels are considered nonrenewable resources. There will be no more once humans use them up.

Coal mines can produce only a certain amount of coal before the supply runs out.

Renewable Energy

Sunlight cannot get used up. It is always available. This makes sunlight a renewable resource. The sun's energy is known as solar energy. People capture solar energy in various ways.

Homes are often built to use natural light.

Letting In Light

People construct buildings to make the most of the sun's heat and light. Many buildings have windows that face south. This gives them more direct sunlight. In cooler months, south-facing windows help heat buildings.

Blocking Light

Sometimes the sun makes buildings too warm. In summer, the sun's path is higher in the sky. Builders block its light with overhangs above windows. This helps buildings stay cool.

Cliff Dwellings

American Indians in the southwest built their homes into south-facing cliffs. The sun warmed the homes in winter. In summer, a rock overhang blocked the high sun. This kept the homes cool.

People have used overhangs to manage sunlight for hundreds of years.

Greenhouses

Many people capture the sun's heat with greenhouses. These structures keep plants warm. They are made of glass or plastic. These clear things let sunlight in. They trap the sun's heat.

Businesses use large greenhouses to grow plants to sell.

Solar ovens may have mirrors shaped like dishes.

Solar Ovens

People also capture the sun's heat with solar ovens. These devices work much like greenhouses. They collect heat and use it to cook food.

Solar stills are sometimes included as emergency supplies in lifeboats.

Solar Stills

Solar stills are devices that produce clean water. They are useful in places with limited drinking water. Solar stills work with the help of the sun.

How a Still Works

First, unclean water goes in an open container. The sun makes the water evaporate. Clean water rises as vapor. This vapor hits a clear covering and becomes liquid. Dirt and salt stay behind. The clean water drips into a different container. It is safe to drink.

Solar Cells

Humans use sunlight to make electricity. They use devices called photovoltaic cells. These are also known as solar cells.

Modern solar cells were invented in the 1950s.

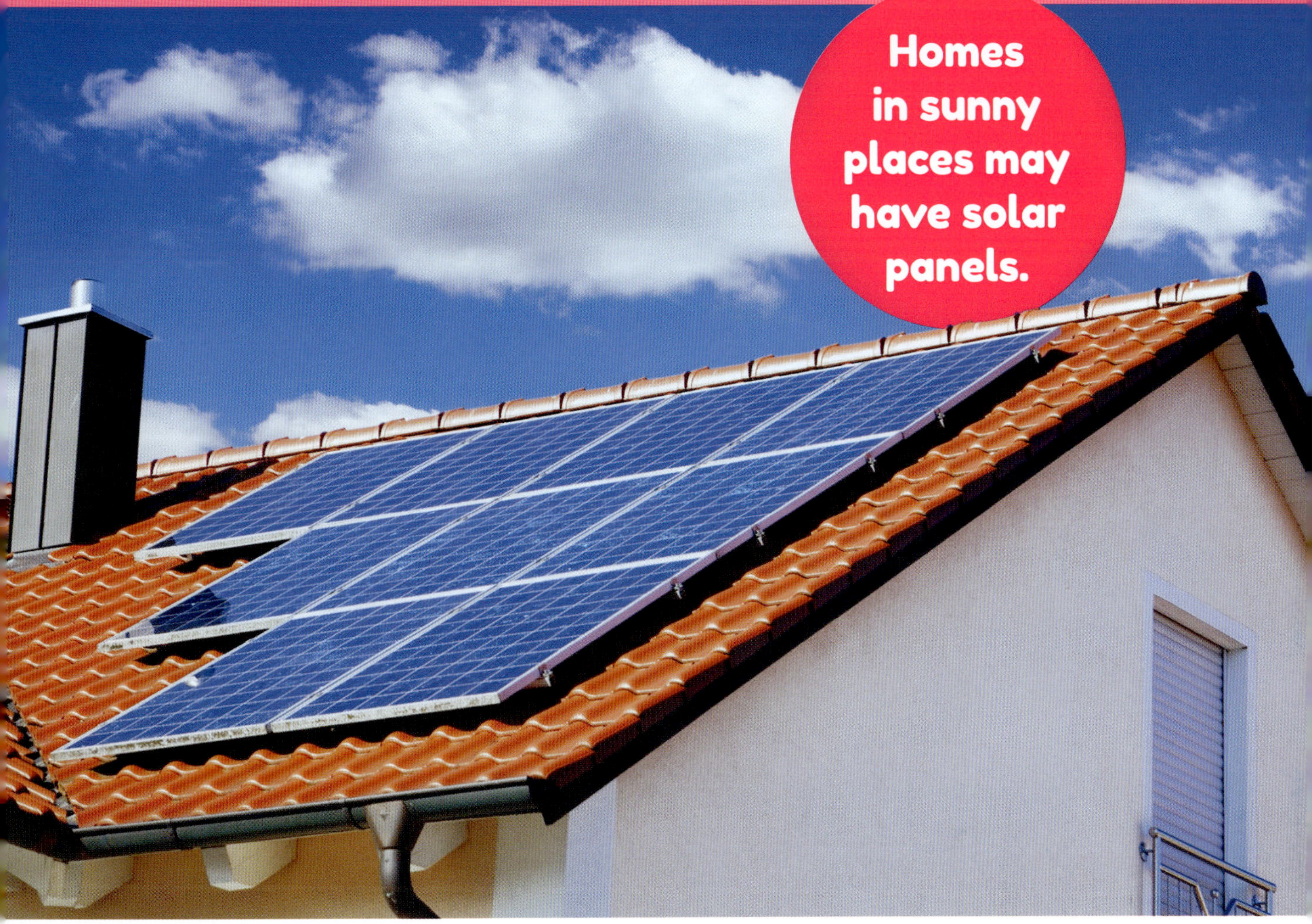

Homes in sunny places may have solar panels.

Solar Panels

A solar panel is a device made up of many solar cells. People can put solar panels on buildings. The panels provide electricity for the building.

FUN FACT!

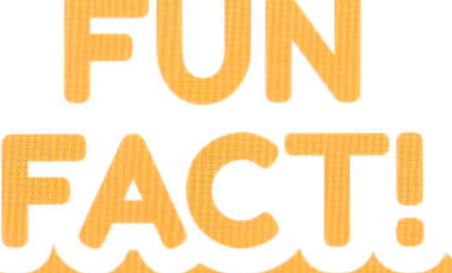

Solar cells can also power cars, planes, and trains.

There is a large CSP plant in Spain.

Sunlight and Mirrors

Concentrated solar power (CSP) is another way to turn sunlight into electricity. CSP uses many mirrors to reflect sunlight onto a receiver. This causes the receiver to heat up.

Spinning Up Electricity

The hot receiver creates steam. Then the steam spins a device called a turbine. The energy of the spinning turbine is turned into electricity.

More Than Enough

Earth receives enough sunlight in one hour to provide the world with electricity for a year. Scientists just need to figure out how to capture it.

The tower of a CSP plant gets amazingly bright and hot.

Visible Light and More

Sunlight is radiation. Some of this radiation is visible. This is the light that allows people to see the world around them. But most of the sun's radiation is not visible to humans.

The sun's heat and light create beautiful weather on Earth.

The Electromagnetic Spectrum

Radio waves, microwaves, and infrared are types of radiation with longer waves. Ultraviolet (UV), X-rays, and gamma rays have shorter waves. In the middle of the spectrum is visible light.

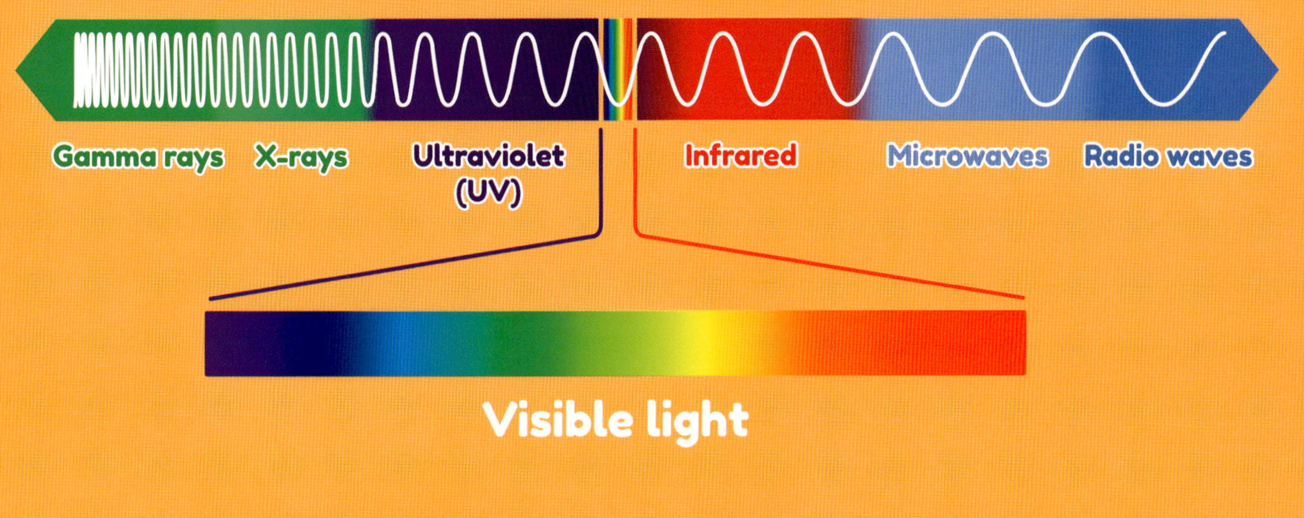

Spectrum of Radiation

Visible and invisible radiation are parts of the electromagnetic spectrum. This is a range of different types of radiation. Each form of radiation travels in waves. Different types of radiation have waves of different lengths.

Special infrared cameras can be used to see energy from this part of the spectrum.

Infrared to Ultraviolet

The sun gives off every type of radiation. But most of the radiation that reaches Earth is infrared and visible light. A smaller percentage is ultraviolet (UV).

Effects of Radiation

Invisible radiation still affects humans. For example, people feel infrared radiation as heat. UV radiation causes sunburn.

A day at the beach can be fun, but people must be careful about UV radiation.

Skin Safety

Most people need some UV radiation. It allows the body to produce vitamin D. This vitamin helps keep bones strong. But too much UV is harmful. Wearing sunscreen helps block UV rays.

People should wear sunscreen when spending time in the sun.

Sunglasses protect the eyes from UV radiation.

Eye Safety

UV radiation can also hurt the eyes. That's why it's important to wear sunglasses on sunny days. People should never look directly at the sun.

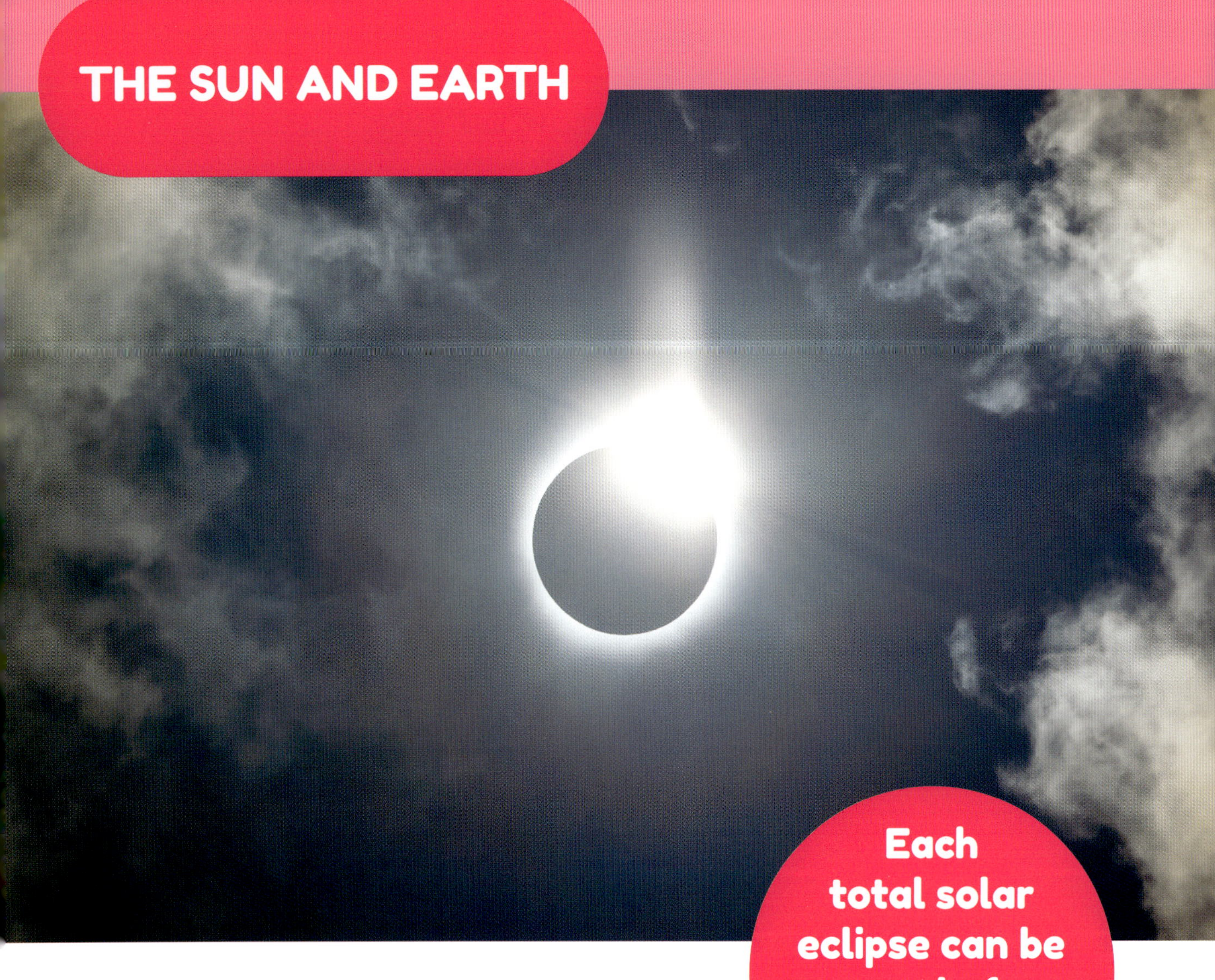

Each total solar eclipse can be seen only from certain places on Earth.

Total Eclipse

The only time it is safe to look at the sun is during a total solar eclipse. This is when the moon passes between Earth and the sun. The moon blocks the sun's entire surface from view.

FUN FACT!

The brief time when the moon completely blocks the sun during an eclipse is called totality.

Eclipse Safety

The bright photosphere is blocked during a total eclipse. This allows people to see the chromosphere and corona. But this moment of total eclipse is brief. Before and after it, looking at the sun is still dangerous.

People must make sure they are wearing approved eclipse glasses for safety.

Space Weather

Solar activity sends huge amounts of radiation and plasma toward Earth. Much of this space weather doesn't affect the planet. This is because Earth has its own magnetic field. It forms a protective bubble.

Earth's magnetic field acts as a shield for the planet.

Early telegraph equipment was affected by space weather in 1859.

Weather Alert

Sometimes space weather does affect Earth. This happens at times when solar activity is high. Strong space weather can break satellites. It also affects radio and power systems.

Bad Weather

In 1859, space weather broke telegraph systems around the world. In 1989, similar space weather caused a power outage in Canada. It affected 6 million people.

Auroras are often seen in the far north.

Auroras

Space weather also creates beauty. It produces displays of light called auroras.

Charged particles in solar wind cause auroras. The particles crash into gases in Earth's atmosphere. This creates glowing colors in the sky.

At the Poles

Auroras are known as Northern Lights and Southern Lights. This is because they usually appear near Earth's North and South Poles.

Weather Forecasting

Scientists forecast space weather with telescopes and other instruments. Some of these instruments are on Earth. Others are on satellites in space. Tracking space weather gives people time to prepare for it. They can also know when to watch for beautiful auroras.

Spacecraft help scientists track solar activity and space weather.

Aurora Colors

Solar wind crashes into gases in Earth's atmosphere to make different colors.

Purple and pink light come from both nitrogen and oxygen.

Blue comes from nitrogen.
Green and red come from oxygen.

Ancient astronomers worked to understand the sun, the moon, and other objects in the sky.

A Great Mystery

Humans have been interested in the sun since ancient times. For thousands of years, they wondered what the sun was. But they didn't have the knowledge or tools to find answers.

Sun Gods

Some believed the sun was a god. Ancient Egyptians believed in a sun god named Re. They thought the sun's movement was Re traveling across the sky in a boat.

Re is often shown with a bird's head and a disk of the sun over him.

Hungry Dragon

Ancient people also wondered about solar eclipses. Some had creative explanations for them. In China, people believed the sun disappeared because a dragon in the sky ate it.

In Chinese mythology, dragons were connected to eclipses.

The idea of the sun circling Earth is called geocentrism.

Ptolemy's Idea

Early scientists slowly learned about the solar system. In the 100s CE, Greek scientist Claudius Ptolemy described it. He thought that Earth was at the center. He believed the sun moved around it. This was a popular belief for hundreds of years.

Thinkers such as Galileo Galilei pushed astronomy forward.

The Scientific Method

A better understanding came during the Scientific Revolution. This was a period of big changes in science. It lasted from the 1500s to the 1700s. People created the scientific method.

This is a system for asking questions, testing ideas, and finding answers.

New Ways of Thinking

Scientists used the scientific method to learn how nature works. Sometimes they proved old beliefs wrong. One of these beliefs was Ptolemy's idea about the sun orbiting Earth.

Galileo drew sunspots that he observed in the early 1600s.

Nicolaus Copernicus

Polish scientist Nicolaus Copernicus proved Ptolemy wrong. Copernicus studied astronomy. In 1543, he wrote about how the solar system worked.

A statue of Nicolaus Copernicus stands in Poland.

Copernicus changed the way scientists thought about the sun.

Copernicus's Idea

Copernicus showed that the sun is at the center of the solar system. Earth and other planets move around the sun. Other scientists built on his ideas. They made more discoveries about space.

FUN FACT!

The study of the sun and its part in the solar system is called heliophysics.

Newton made many scientific discoveries.

Isaac Newton

Isaac Newton was also part of the Scientific Revolution. He was an English scientist. In the 1600s, Newton experimented with prisms. A prism is a clear object with at least one angled side.

Newton's Findings

Newton observed sunlight passing through a prism. He saw that light bends and splits into the colors of the rainbow. Newton's work helped other scientists discover more about light.

Newton showed that white light is made up of seven colors.

Solar Filters

Modern solar telescopes have special filters. The filters let only a small amount of sunlight pass through. This protects the viewer's eyes.

Telescopes

People invented telescopes in the 1600s. These tools let scientists observe the sun in greater detail. They could now study solar features such as sunspots.

Hans Lippershey is believed to be the inventor of the telescope.

Types of Telescopes

Refracting telescopes bend light with lenses.
Reflecting telescopes reflect light with mirrors.

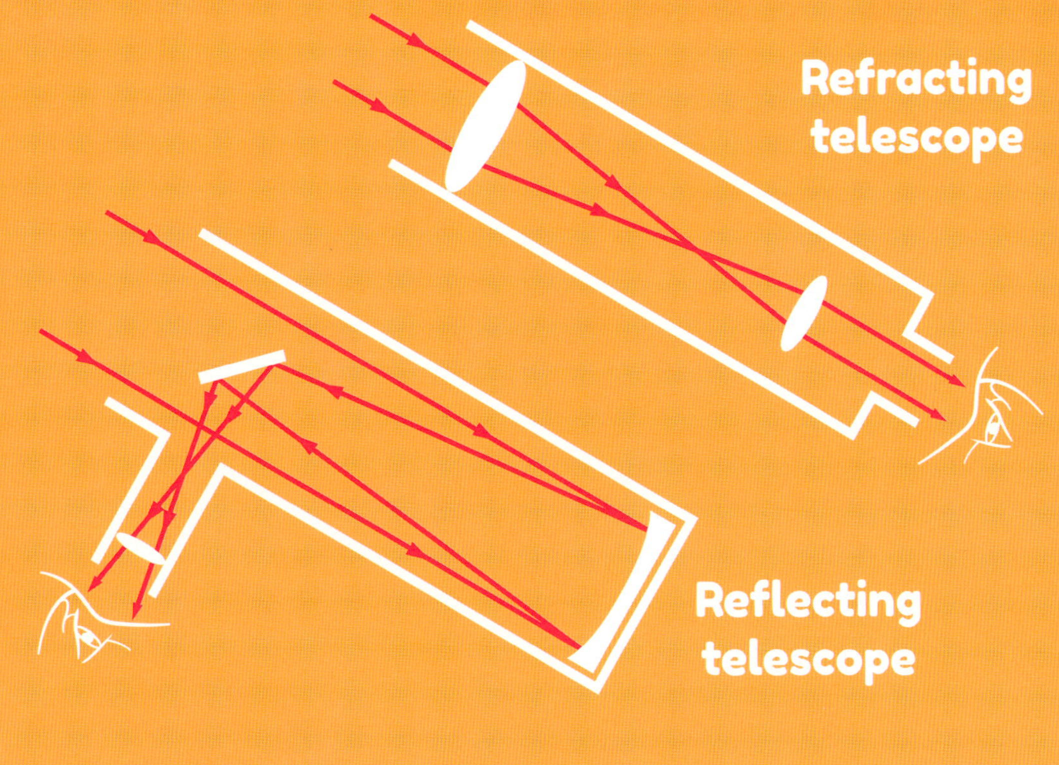

Types of Telescopes

Some telescopes use lenses to bend incoming light. Other telescopes use mirrors to reflect incoming light. In both cases, the telescope creates a clear image. The viewer can see this image through an eyepiece.

A scientist uses an early spectroscope.

Spectroscope

In the 1800s, scientists invented the spectroscope. This instrument separates visible light into different colors. It also separates invisible radiation into different types. These include infrared and UV radiation.

Sun Data

Spectroscopes give scientists data about the sun. For example, a spectroscope can show differences in temperature. It can also show which chemical elements make up the sun.

Lines in the spectrum of light can show the elements that are in a star.

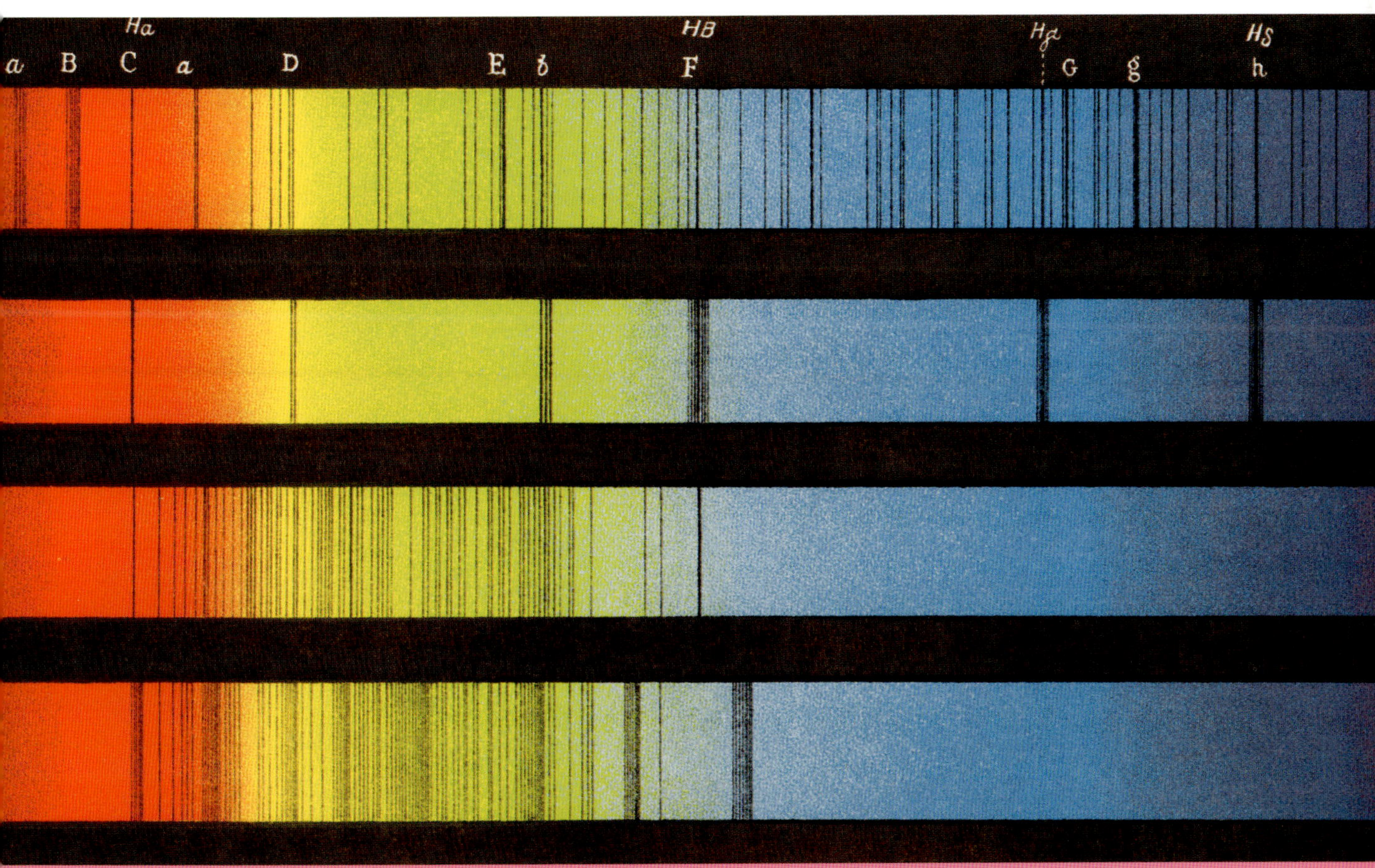

Coronagraph

Astronomers invented the coronagraph in 1930. This is a telescope with a circular screen. The screen blocks the photosphere. This allows the viewer to study the corona.

A coronagraph allows scientists to see what's happening in the corona.

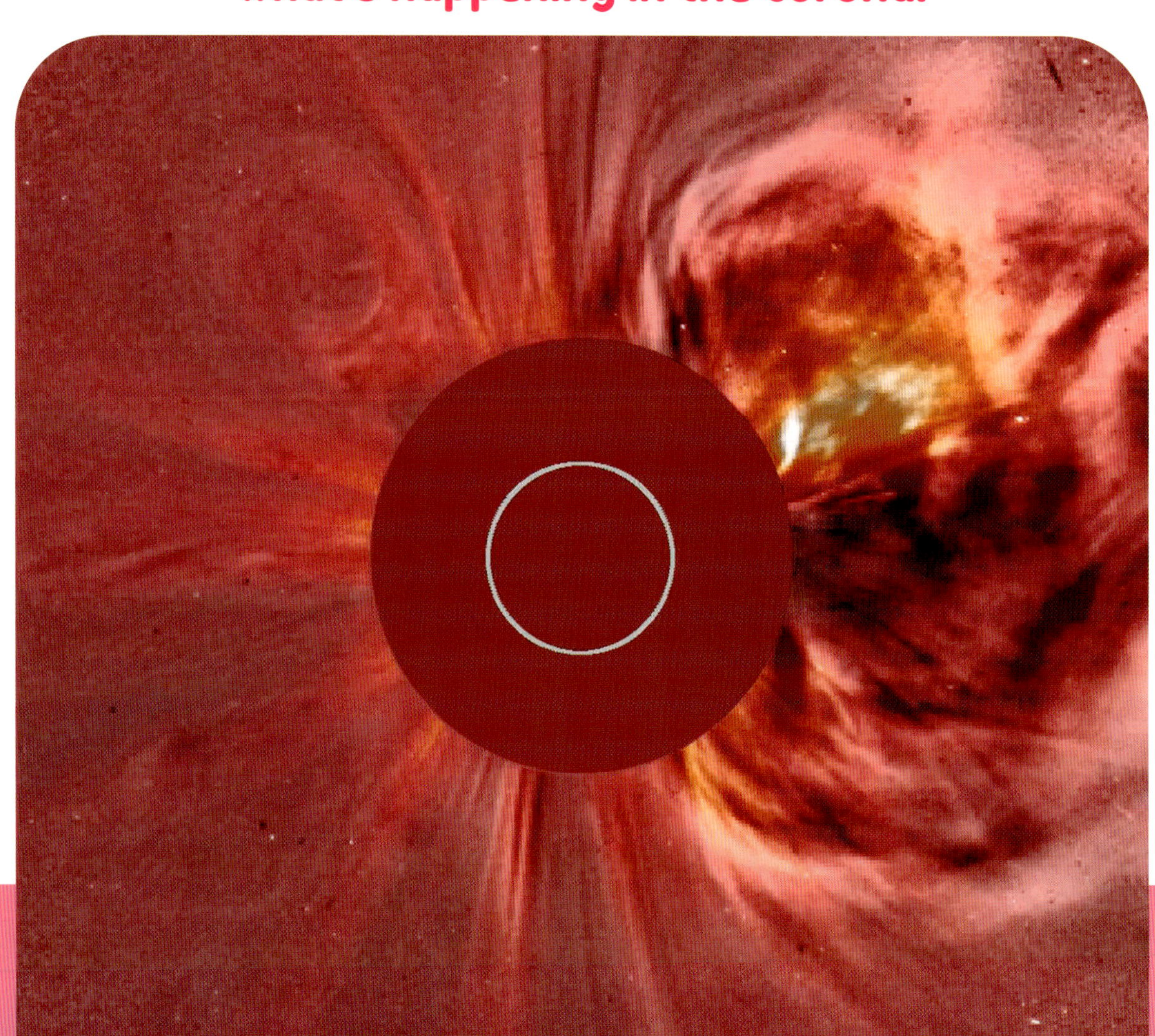

Radio telescopes often look like large satellite dishes.

Radio Telescopes and Beyond

The 1930s also brought the first radio telescope. This tool detects radio waves produced by the sun. People later invented telescopes that detect other kinds of invisible radiation.

FUN FACT!

The world's largest solar telescope is in Hawaii. It is able to detect the sun's magnetic field.

Putting telescopes in space gives them a much clearer view.

Studying with Spacecraft

Sunlight doesn't move straight through Earth's atmosphere. Some of it gets bent or blocked by particles. This is known as atmospheric distortion. It can make the view blurry through telescopes. One solution is to put telescopes in space, beyond Earth's atmosphere.

Beyond the Atmosphere

The National Aeronautics and Space Administration (NASA) runs many US space missions. NASA began launching spacecraft to study the sun in the 1960s. These spacecraft hold telescopes and other instruments. They send data back to Earth.

Space telescopes must be sturdy to survive a forceful rocket launch.

Skylab

In 1973, NASA launched America's first space station. This was Skylab. Astronauts lived there for months at a time. One of their goals was to learn more about the sun.

Skylab astronaut Owen Garriott works at the telescope controls.

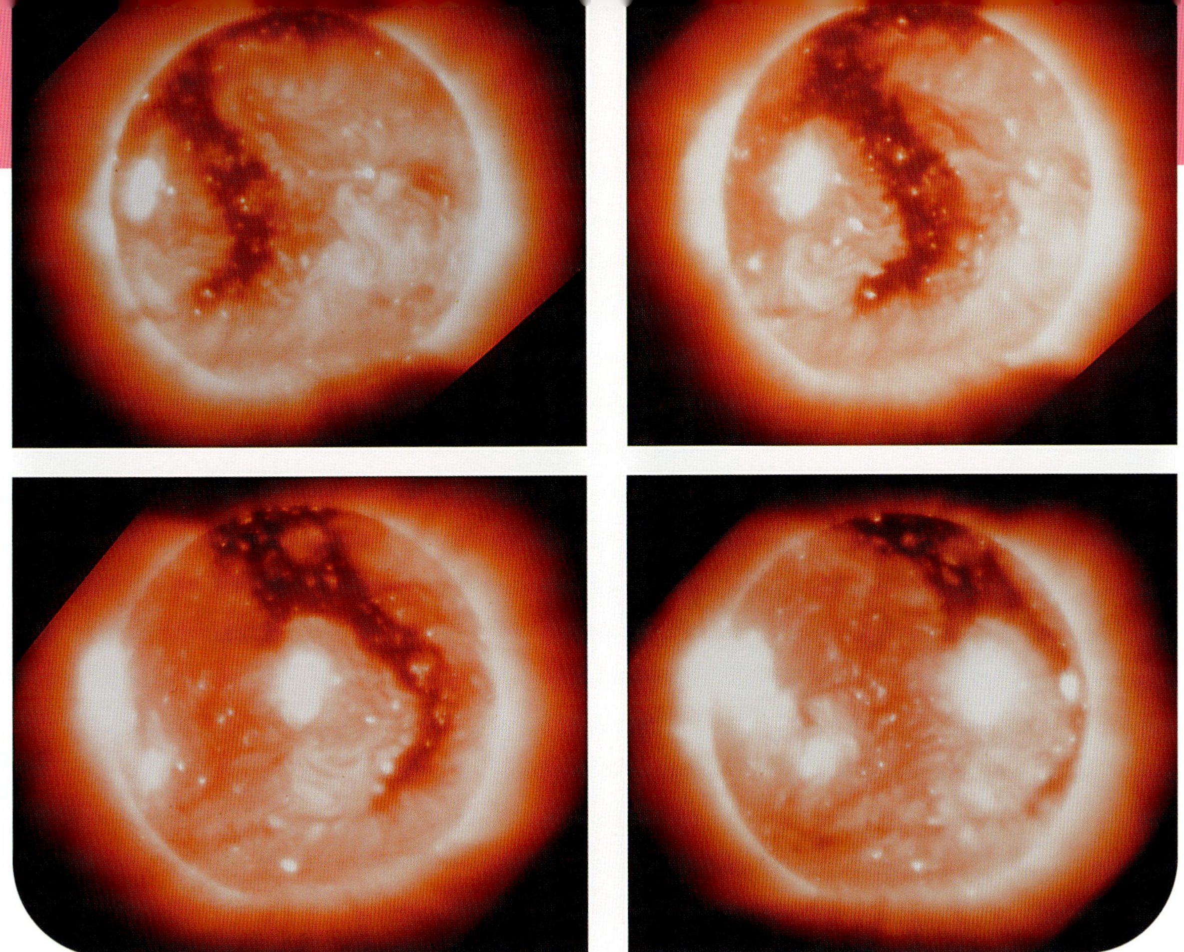

Skylab astronauts took these X-ray images of the sun.

Coronal Discoveries

Skylab astronauts used telescopes to capture images of the sun. X-ray telescopes provided the first images of the sun's coronal holes. These are areas where the corona appears dark. They mark openings in the sun's magnetic field. Solar wind escapes the sun at coronal holes.

The SMM gathered new data about the corona.

SMM

NASA launched the Solar Maximum Mission (SMM) in 1980. This mission took place during a time of high solar activity. The goal of the SMM was to learn more about solar flares and sunspots.

Flares and Spots

The SMM studied radiation produced by solar flares. The SMM also made an important discovery about sunspots. It found that dark sunspots are surrounded by brighter areas. This means the sun is brighter overall when there are more sunspots.

An astronaut, *lower right*, works on the SMM satellite in orbit.

SOHO

In 1995, NASA worked with the European Space Agency (ESA). Together, they launched the SOHO satellite. SOHO stands for Solar and Heliospheric Observatory. SOHO's goal was to study the sun's layers and the solar wind.

Scientists prepared SOHO for launch in November 1995.

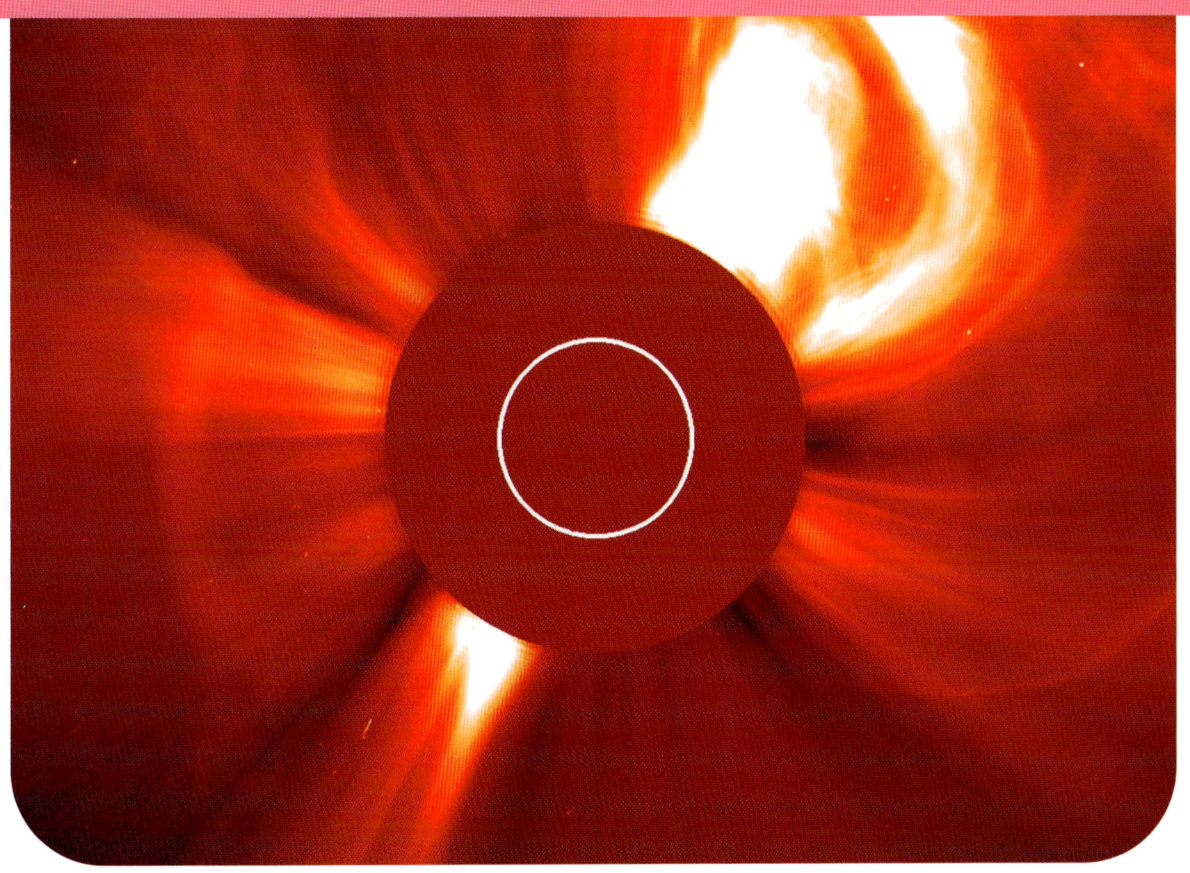

SOHO captured an image of a large CME in 2002.

Winds and Weather

SOHO discovered solar tornadoes. They are made of swirling plasma. SOHO studies this and other solar activity. This allows scientists to forecast space weather.

FUN FACT!

SOHO's mission was supposed to end in 1998. But it remained active in 2025.

STEREO

In 2006, NASA launched twin spacecraft called STEREO A and B. STEREO stands for Solar Terrestrial Relations Observatory. The two spacecraft orbited the sun alongside Earth. One of their goals was to learn more about CMEs.

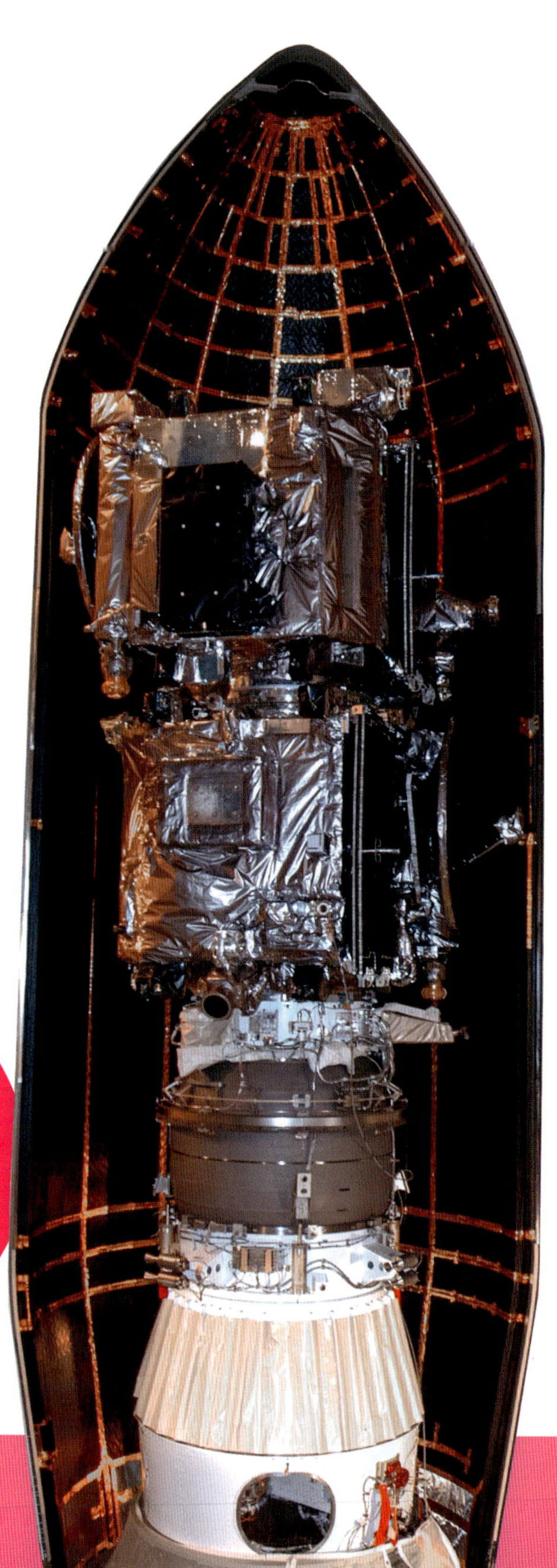

STEREO A sat on top of STEREO B inside the rocket.

3D Sun

The STEREO spacecraft took images of the sun from different angles. Then NASA combined the images. This produced 3D images. Scientists could watch CMEs as they moved through space. This helped them forecast any effects on Earth.

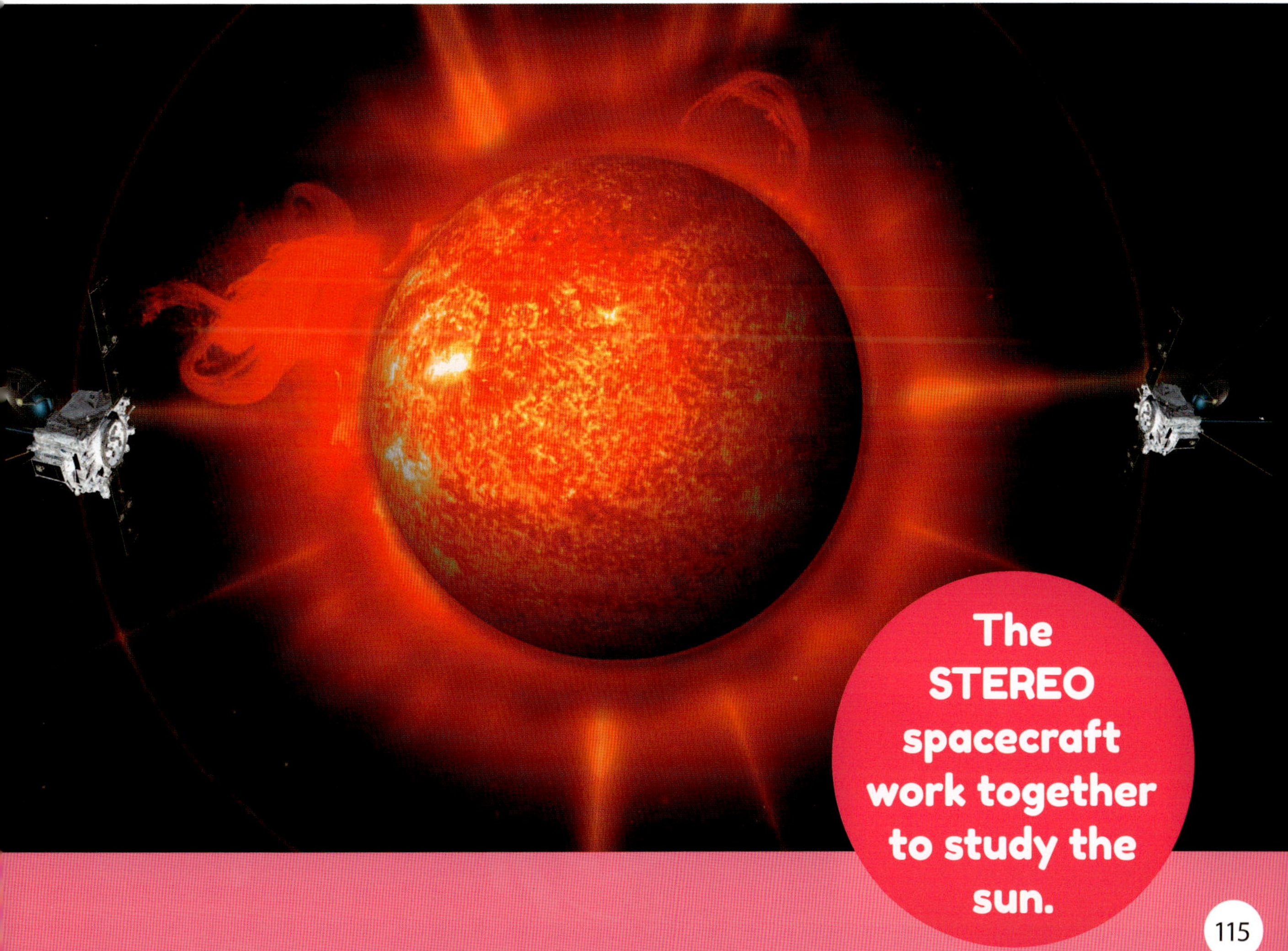

The STEREO spacecraft work together to study the sun.

Solar Orbiter

NASA and the ESA worked together again in 2020. That year, they launched the Solar Orbiter. This spacecraft set out to learn more about solar activity.

Engineers work on the Solar Orbiter before launch.

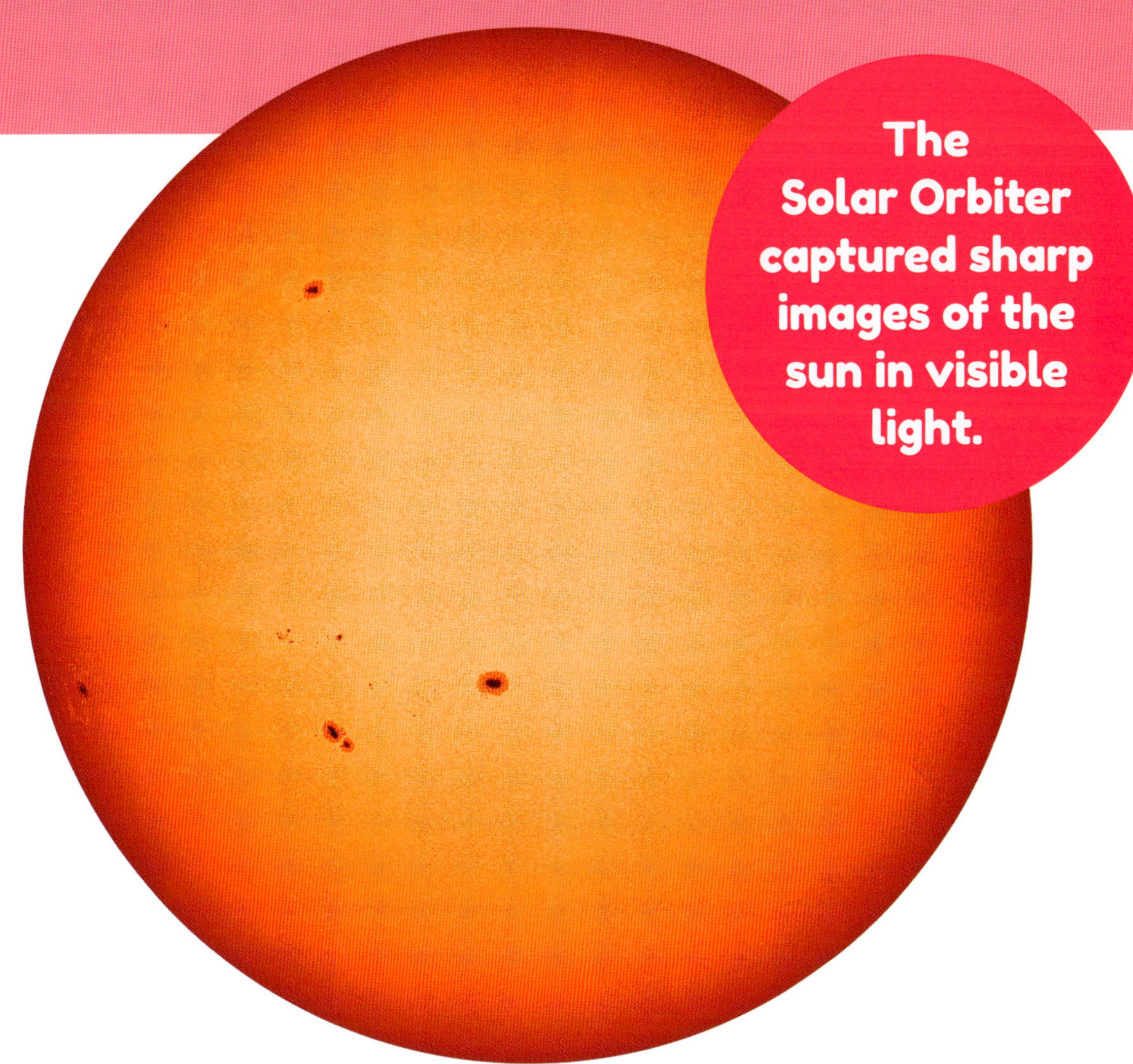

The Solar Orbiter captured sharp images of the sun in visible light.

Solar Close-Ups

In its first year, the Solar Orbiter made history. It delivered the closest images ever taken of the sun. It also produced the clearest image yet of the sun's south pole.

FUN FACT!

The Solar Orbiter's images of the sun revealed mini solar flares. Scientists named them campfires.

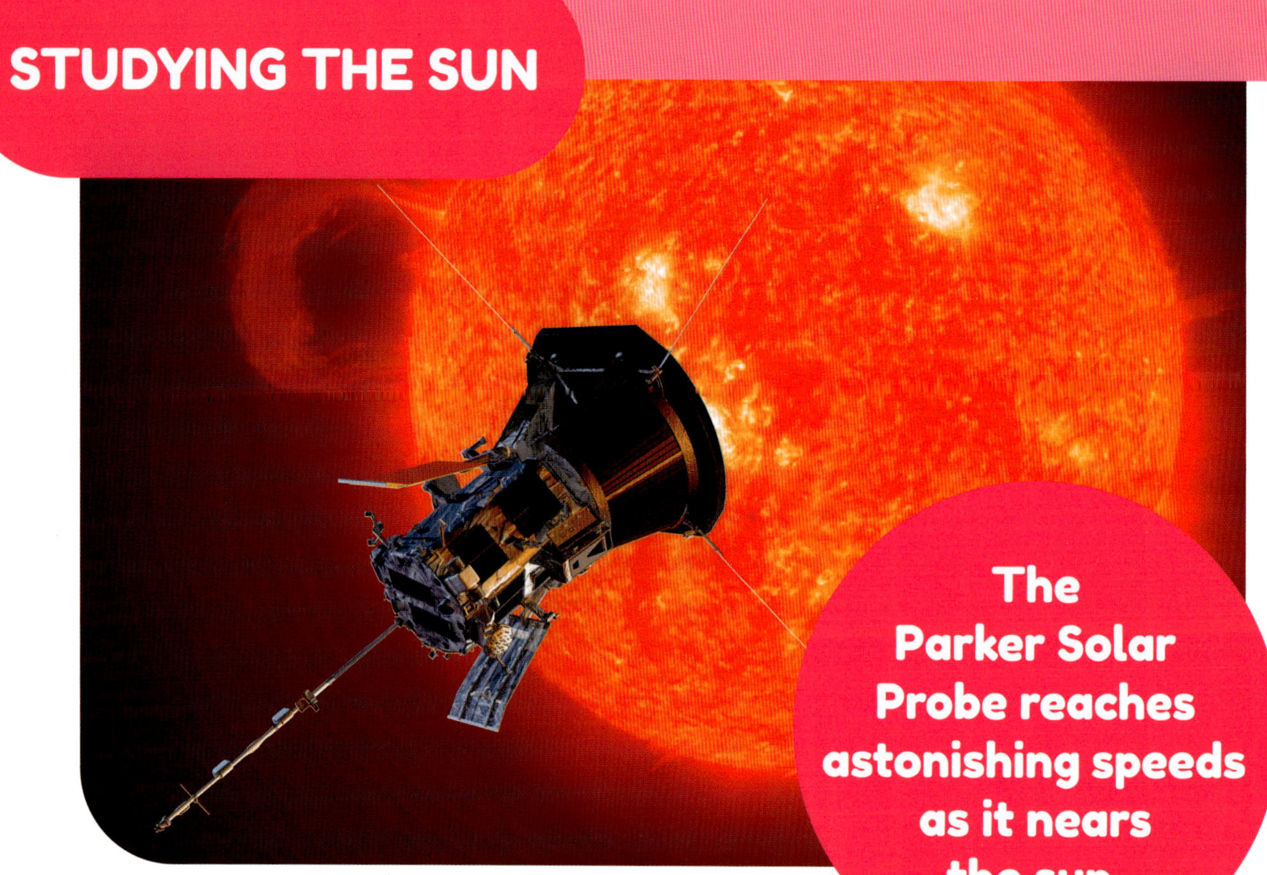

The Parker Solar Probe reaches astonishing speeds as it nears the sun.

Parker Solar Probe

NASA's Parker Solar Probe launched in 2018. Its goal was to get very close to the sun's surface. Scientists hoped the mission would answer questions about the corona and solar wind.

Record Breaker

In 2021, the Parker Solar Probe became the first spacecraft to fly through the corona.

And in 2024, it traveled within 3.8 million miles (6.1 million km) of the sun. This is the closest any spacecraft has come to the sun.

Heat Shield

A thick carbon shield protects the Parker Solar Probe from the sun's heat. The shield can resist temperatures of 2,600 degrees Fahrenheit (1,427°C).

Close to the Sun

The Parker Solar Probe travels much closer to the sun than any of the planets.

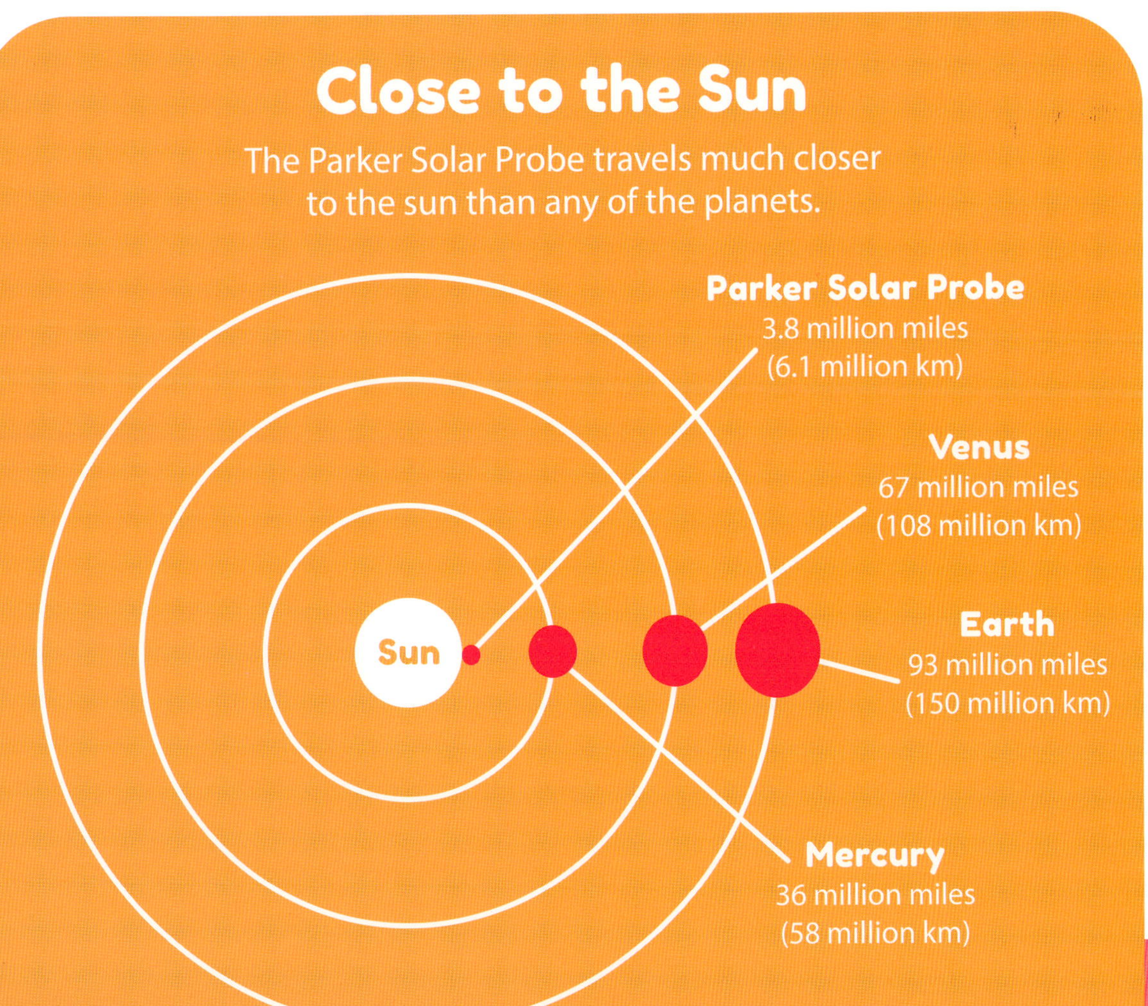

Billions to Go

The sun will provide heat and light for a very long time. But like all stars, it will burn out. Scientists think this will happen in about 5 billion years.

As with all stars, the sun has a limited lifespan.

More Nuclear Fusion

The sun is using up hydrogen over time. The core will become mostly helium. It will heat up, and more nuclear fusion will happen. This extra energy will make the sun grow.

Heat Wave

When the sun grows, the outer parts of the solar system will warm up. The moons of Jupiter and Saturn could become warm enough to support life.

As the sun grows, it may grow all the way to Earth's orbit.

Growing and Cooling

The sun will reach 200 times its current size. It will swallow Mercury, Venus, and possibly Earth. As the sun grows, its surface will cool. This will turn the sun a reddish color.

Red Giant

At this point, the sun will be a red giant. This is a star nearing the end of its life. The sun's core will get hotter. It will reach about 180 million degrees Fahrenheit (100 million°C). Helium in the core will fuse into the element carbon.

The sun will spend about 1 billion years as a red giant.

Stars, Not Planets

Planetary nebulae have nothing to do with planets. They were named by early astronomers who thought they looked like planets.

Planetary Nebula

One day, the sun will throw off its outer layers. This will create a cloud of gas and dust called a planetary nebula. This is the shortest stage of the sun's life cycle. It will last only about 10,000 years.

Planetary nebulae can be seen through telescopes.

Life Cycle of the Sun

The sun will remain a yellow dwarf star for about 5 billion more years. Then it will become a red giant, planetary nebula, and white dwarf.

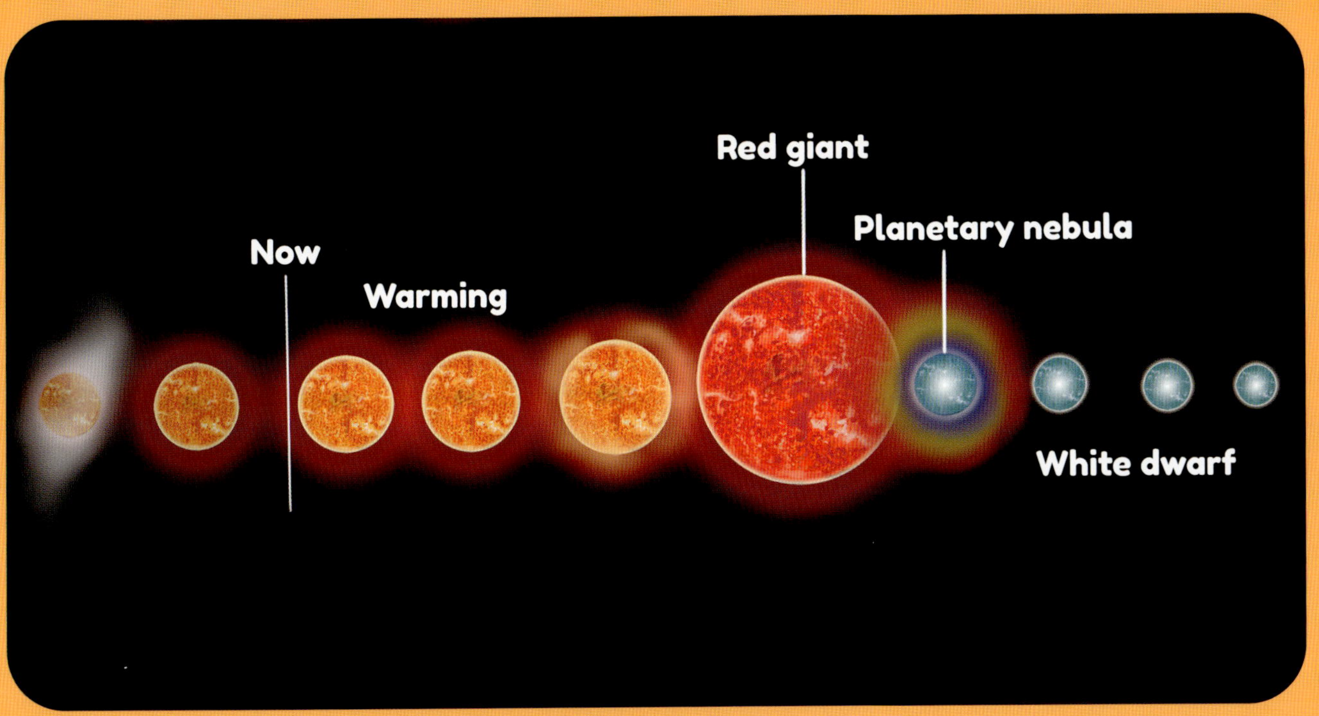

White Dwarf

After the nebula stage, only the sun's carbon core will remain. The sun will be a white dwarf. This is a dim star about the size of Earth. Nuclear fusion will stop. The sun will be at the end of its long life.

GLOSSARY

astronomy
The study of objects in space.

atmosphere
The gases that surround an object in space.

atom
The basic building block of all matter in the universe.

concentrated
Happening in a small space.

dense
Having a high mass in a given amount of space.

equator
An imaginary circle halfway between Earth's North and South Poles.

erupt
To explode or burst.

forecast
To guess something is likely to happen based on data.

hemisphere
One half of Earth.

invisible
Not able to be seen.

magnetic field
An area in which magnetic forces are present.

mass
The amount of matter in an object.

mission
A task or job.

particle
A tiny piece of something.

satellite
A spacecraft that orbits an object in space, usually Earth.

3D
Having depth in addition to length and width.

tilted
At an angle instead of straight.

TO LEARN MORE

More Books to Read

Allan, Sophie. *The Solar System*. DK, 2023.

Huddleston, Emma. *Explore the Sun*. Abdo, 2022.

Marquardt, Meg. *Space*. Abdo, 2025.

Online Resources

To learn more about the sun, please visit **abdobooklinks.com** or scan this QR code. These links are routinely monitored and updated to provide the most current information available.

PHOTO CREDITS

Cover Photos: Adobe Stock, front; Shutterstock Images, back
Interior Photos: Shutterstock Images, 1, 3, 4, 5, 6, 7, 8, 9, 11, 13, 14, 16, 17 (atoms), 19, 23, 24, 26, 29 (top), 29 (bottom), 30, 32, 36, 44, 45, 47 (top), 47 (bottom), 50, 53 (bottom), 56 (top), 56 (bottom), 58, 59, 60, 61, 62, 65, 67 (top), 67 (bottom), 69, 72, 73, 75 (top), 75 (bottom), 80, 81, 84, 85 (bottom), 86 (bottom), 88–89, 91, 100 (top), 101, 105, 119 (top), 120, 121 (bottom), 124 (bottom); Romanenko Alexey/Shutterstock Images, 10; Jurik Peter/Shutterstock Images, 12; Andrea Danti/Shutterstock Images, 15; Red Line Editorial, 17 (pie chart), 119 (bottom); Paul Wootton/Science Source, 18; Claus Lunau/Science Source, 20, 22; Monica Schroeder/Science Source, 21; T. Rimmele (NSO), M.Hanna, NOAO/AURA/NSF/Science Source, 25; Miguel Claro/Science Source, 27; NASA, 28, 33, 34, 35, 37, 38, 39, 42, 43, 46, 104, 107, 108, 109, 111, 112, 115, 118; John Chumack/Science Source, 31; Judah Santiago/Shutterstock Images, 40; NASA/Science Source, 41, 110; Mark Garlick/Science Source, 48, 52; Melnikov Dmitriy/Shutterstock Images, 49; Olga Kuzmina/Shutterstock Images, 51; Adobe Stock, 53 (top); Mikkel Juul Jensen/Science Source, 54; Tim Brown/Science Source, 55; Nick Starichenko/Shutterstock Images, 57; Igor Hotinsky/Shutterstock Images, 63; Zack Frank/Shutterstock Images, 64; VIS Fine Art/Shutterstock Images, 66; Zigmunds Dizgalvis/Shutterstock Images, 68; Marcus Harrison-outdoors/Alamy, 70; DK Images/Science Source, 71; Joseph Creamer/Shutterstock Images, 74; Monkey Business Images/Shutterstock Images, 76; Oleksandr Panasovskyi/Shutterstock Images, 77; Ivan Smuk/Shutterstock Images, 78; iStockphoto, 79; Thomas Roell/Shutterstock Images, 82; Fethi Belaid/AFP/Getty Images, 83; Universal History Archive/Universal Images Group/Getty Images, 85 (top), 90; Nemes Laszlo/Science Source, 86 (top); NOAA, 87; Sanit Fuangnakhon/Shutterstock Images, 92; Ann Ronan Pictures/Print Collector/Hulton Archive/Getty Images, 93, 95; Fine Art Images/Heritage Images/Hulton Fine Art Collection/Getty Images, 94; Lukasz Janyst/Shutterstock Images, 96; Oxford Science Archive/Print Collector/Hulton Archive/Getty Images, 97; Popperfoto/Getty Images, 98; Apic/Hulton Archive/Getty Images, 99; Bettmann/Getty Images, 100 (bottom); Science Source, 102; David Parker/Science Source, 103; Dima Zel/Shutterstock Images, 106; SOHO/ESA & NASA, 113; George Shelton/NASA, 114; Ben Smegelsky/NASA, 116; ESA & NASA, 117; Sergey Mironov/Shutterstock Images, 121 (top); European Southern Observatory/Science Source, 122; Tomasz Dabrowski/Stocktrek Images/Science Source, 123; Fath Yusuf Iskhaqy/Shutterstock Images, 124 (top); Spencer Sutton/Science Source, 125